# Picking Up
# the Pieces

# Picking Up the Pieces

Two Accounts

of a Psychoanalytic

Journey

**Fayek Nakhla, M.D.**

**Grace Jackson**

Yale University Press
New Haven and London

Published with assistance from the Kingsley Trust
Association Publication Fund established by the
Scroll and Key Society of Yale College.
Designed by Deborah Dutton.
Set in Melior type and Zapf International display type
by DEKR Corp., Woburn, Massachusetts.
Printed in the United States of America by Vail-Ballou
Press, Binghamton, New York.

Library of Congress Cataloging-in-Publication Data

Nakhla, Fayek, 1933–
    Picking up the pieces : two accounts of a psychoanalytic journey /
Fayek Nakhla, Grace Jackson.
        p.     cm.
    Includes bibliographical references and index.
    ISBN 0–300–05653–2
    1. Psychoanalysis—Case studies.   2. Selflessness (Psychology)—
Case studies.   3. Psychotherapist and patient—Case studies.
4. Nakhla, Fayek, 1933–    .  5. Jackson, Grace, 1949–
I. Jackson, Grace, 1949–    .  II. Title.
RC509.8.N35   1993
616.89′17—dc20                        93-1304
                                                CIP

A catalogue record for this book is available from the
British Library.

The paper in this book meets the guidelines for
permanence and durability of the Committee on
Production Guidelines for Book Longevity of the
Council on Library Resources.

10 9 8 7 6 5 4 3 2 1

In psychology it must be said that the infant falls to pieces unless held together, and physical care is psychological care at these stages.
—D. W. Winnicott, *Human Nature*

For Grace's parents, her sisters, and her husband

# Contents

# Foreword

Joyce McDougall

This is a unique book. There are many full-length case studies of patients suffering from mental illness, and even a few published accounts on which patient and therapist worked together. This book, in which both analyst and analysand tell the story of their mutual enterprise from their individual viewpoints, also provides a detailed clinical account of the treatment process.

The reader is led not only through the vivid and gripping experience of Grace Jackson's psychological suffering and terror but also through Fayek Nakhla's distress and bewilderment as he attempted to understand and identify with his patient's extreme mental pain and conflict.

Through Grace's consistent diary writing we are given a privileged insight into her private world; she exhibits an

extraordinary ability to describe her frightening mental confusion in lucid detail.

At the same time Dr. Nakhla's constant search for understanding, through his awareness of his own psychic
pain, led him to construct thought-provoking and carefully
researched formulations of the complex clinical phenomena he was experiencing with his patient. Furthermore, he
shares with us the challenge that this unusual experience
presented from the viewpoint of technical management.

The creative endeavors of Grace Jackson and Fayek
Nakhla may lead certain clinicians to question whether the
supremely delicate therapeutic adventure they shared is to
be considered psychoanalysis. It is evident that the ordinary analytic technique used in treating neurotic states and
symptoms would be totally inadequate to a pre-object fu-
sional state, such as Grace experienced, in which violent
action and self-inflicted bodily harm were essential means
of communication.

The analyst's affective responses to his analysand's
mute transmission of her suffering led him to listen acutely
to his own countertransference experience and to search
for intuitive solutions to the difficult task of containing and
interpreting the meaning of her overwhelming mental pain.

Thanks to the two accounts of this psychoanalytic journey, we are given a truer picture of the therapeutic relationship and the intricacies of transference and countertransference interactions. The reader will be impressed by
the candor of both participants, particularly since this al-
lows one to understand the personal distress of each as
well as the intimate learning experience involved.

An intriguing feature of Dr. Nakhla's creativity is re-
vealed in his making use of his extensive experience with
family therapy by introducing members of Grace's family
into her treatment at a crucial moment. Thus mother and

daughter were able to enter into an inaugural relationship based on mutual appreciation and understanding.

This book is an important piece of research in that the analyst had to undertake major departures from accepted psychoanalytic technique, involving inevitable errors and risking his patient's bodily integrity in the service of her psychic and physical survival. The reader cannot fail to admire Dr. Nakhla's courage and devotion, coupled with a high level of skill and self-discipline, in which no breach of ethical values, no abuse, and no exploitation of his patient occurred.

In the same vein, we can appreciate Grace Jackson's struggle with psychotic terror coupled with indomitable courage to continue her painful but rewarding psychoanalytic journey. In addition, both authors display considerable literary skill in the frank exploration of their feelings throughout this challenging experience.

Apart from its appeal to the general reader, this book has evident professional value. It not only provides an original addition to the growing body of research literature into the theoretical understanding and treatment of patients in the grip of severely regressed and psychotic states but at the same time contributes to a deeper understanding of the unconscious fantasies and anxieties that underlie less extreme forms of pathology. Indeed, this unique account may throw light on the intimate core of everyone's private madness.

# Acknowledgments

I wish to thank the staff of Brookdale Hospital for providing me with a strong foundation of support during Grace's treatment. I knew that I always had a safety net—that at any moment I could fall back on hospital admission for Grace. Later, as I was writing the book, I was gratified to receive the interest and encouragement of several colleagues at Brookdale, in particular the members of the Faculty Psychotherapy Study Group, who read and made helpful comments about portions of the manuscript.

My wife, Yvette, provided the caring environment I needed during this long process. I treasure the patience with which she endured the sacrifices of our weekend time together, and the faith she had in this endeavor from its inception. She has my gratitude, and my love.

F. N.


We are indebted to Joyce McDougall, of the Paris Psychoanalytical Society, who first suggested that this therapeutic venture be made into a book. Her enthusiasm helped launch the project, and we continued to consult her during her frequent visits to New York. Her thoughtful suggestions and probing questions were instrumental in shaping the book.

F. N.

G. J.

# Picking Up
# the Pieces

# Introduction

(Dr. Nakhla)

o

## Writing the Book

Grace Jackson was a precocious child with a highly developed intellect.* She was viewed as a model child by her parents and teachers. From an early age, however, she sensed that "something was not right" with her, and in time she came to struggle with her sense of identity: the feeling that she did not exist as a person and was somehow not real. In her mid-twenties, she turned to psychoanalysis in her attempt to find herself. This book is the story of the first three and a half years of treatment, which began in 1973 and lasted sixteen years in all. The account

* Grace Jackson is a pseudonym.

1

ends with Grace's emergence from her life-and-death struggles and deep regression into the beginnings of a distinct sense of a true and separate self.

The writing began in 1988, in the final year of treatment, and was an important and integral part of the therapy. In the spring of that year, I showed Grace a paper in Italian, "I precursori dell'oggetto e dei fenomeni transizionali" (Precursors of the transitional object and transitional phenomena), which I had received from its author, the analyst Renata Gaddini, and asked her if she could translate a letter from Winnicott that was an appendix to it. She had been studying Italian for a couple of years and was eager to do it. Then she wanted to know why I was reading the paper. Her question took me by surprise, and without thinking I answered that I had been trying to understand her wrist cutting and blood as a transitional object and I told her about Gaddini's notion of precursors to the transitional object—the child's security blanket. Grace became curious and suggested that she translate the whole paper, not just the letter. She asked if I had something by Winnicott to read that would help her with the translation, and I gave her "Playing and Reality."

As Grace became aware of my attempts to understand and formulate aspects of the clinical experience from a theoretical point of view, her interest was excited. She asked, "What did happen? When I first came to see you I didn't feel I had a body; now I believe I do. How did that come about? I suppose it's all in my diary. But how to make sense of that, give it a form?" I pressed her: Did she really want to understand what happened? She said, "Of course, unless you don't think I should." I felt that it would be useful for her, and also that she might be able to tell me things I did not understand or was unaware of. After all, I told her, it was really her experience.

This brought into focus a tentative idea I had had of writing about Grace and our therapeutic venture. Three years earlier, I had consulted with the French analyst Joyce McDougall, not to get help with Grace's treatment but to discuss what I knew had been an unusual clinical experience. McDougall was very interested and supportive, and encouraged me to write about it, knowing that I had kept detailed notes. As we were discussing the journals that might publish such an article, she suggested that it might be easier and more meaningful to write a book than to try to reduce or excerpt the experience as an article. After that, I began thinking about a book, but a book that Grace and I would write together. In fact, I thought of it as essentially Grace's book, to which I would contribute in some way; she had kept an extensive diary for many years, and I had always thought that she might someday use it to write about her experience.

Pursuing the idea of working together to try and understand what happened, I suggested to Grace that we write about it separately—I using my notes, she her diary. To give some framework to this writing, I divided the first few years into four phases. The book ultimately covered the first three and a half years of treatment—the time during which regression took place.

At first, we continued to meet twice a week in my office. Although in my mind the writing was firmly connected with the idea of a book, I also felt that it was valuable therapeutically. Sharing the accounts of the early and turbulent period of treatment brought tremendous excitement but also tremendous anxiety and, as we looked back, a sense of loss for both of us. I had been worried that reliving what she had been through would be upsetting and disruptive for Grace; as it turned out, it was much more difficult for me. Many things were painful or frightening to remember, and I often found myself near tears. I recognized, of course, that only now that I had survived could I afford to experience these emotions; nevertheless, I was surprised.

I had thought of the writing as a terminal phase of therapy and considered it important to maintain the framework of the treatment situation. As the months passed, however, I became more comfortable and settled with what Grace and I were accomplishing, and was less certain about the nature of our relationship and the need for continued treatment. I wondered if Grace was communicating similar feelings when, giving me a check, she quoted Winnicott's dedication of "Playing and Reality": "To my patients who have paid to teach me." I decided to bring up the issue of termination. We would have a different relationship, I explained, working together and writing; and she wouldn't be paying me. Grace said, "What an idea: radical. It never occurred to me. The end of treatment and writing the story were entirely bound up together, were the same thing." Yet, she told me later, "that was what I wanted more than anything." I said, "You must have thought of the end of treatment." "Yes, but in terms of the book being written, finished; although this also makes sense." I told her that treatments do end and explained that although the patient usually brings it up, the decision is mutual. Usually a date is set, a few months ahead. Did she want to set a date? Grace said it didn't make sense to her to stop and discuss ending the sessions or to set what seemed an arbitrary date. Instead, she suggested that we just try stopping.

I agreed, and after some discussion we decided, for practical reasons (for example, she had a computer we could work on), to meet at her house one morning a week. Our analytic relationship and its framework abruptly changed. The context of the relationship expanded and in some ways became more complex; now Grace was relating to me as a real person in an ordinary life situation.

Although the treatment account conveys the transformations in me as I responded to the intense feelings and anxieties I encountered, and to the clinical concepts that guided my work, many of my ideas crystallized and were formulated only during the writing of the book. I came to comprehend more fully that in the analytic relationship I had primarily been a real object rather than a transference object. There was a new object relation and a new beginning, in which aspects of the earliest developmental needs and conflicts were re-created. I had been "the first really reliable object" (Reich, 1958), and, as Bergmann (1988) says in his paper on termination of analysis, the analyst's image acquires for the patient a psychic importance equivalent to that of the original parents.

For Grace, the writing meant that the dream of someone reading her diary, making sense of it, telling her who she was in a concrete way, was to be realized. But this was also her fear: "What if what he saw in my diary wasn't me, wasn't who or what he thought. What if I had given him a completely wrong picture of myself. What if what I wrote wasn't 'right'?"[1] But in the end she said of the writing:

> The "I" that I saw as I read through my diary seemed
> crazy, out of control, in a way that at the time I had
> not realized or understood. It was often difficult reliv-
> ing this: it was me and not me. What was striking,
> and completely new, for me listening to the doctor
> was the idea that there could be a structure and con-
> text for my experience. I was not isolated, it was not
> meaningless outside me, was not random, but had a

1. Klauber's (1987) ideas about the phenomenon he termed "illusion" (particularly as outlined in his essays "The Role of Illusion
in Psychoanalytic Cure" and "Truth and Illusion in the Patient's
Symptoms") illuminate many facets of this analytic encounter, especially Grace's emotional courage to live beyond reality.

plot, and could perhaps be communicated to someone else.

I became aware, too, of the doctor's devotion, of how I had been held by him. Writing the book seemed to be a psychic holding, as opposed to the years of physical holding. He had once made a reference to "everything we have been through together." At the time this had made no sense to me; now I began to understand and appreciate what it meant.[2]

About six months after we stopped meeting in my office, we had a first draft of the first half of the book. Four and a half years after my first meeting with McDougall, I met with her again and gave her a copy of the manuscript, reminding her that it was she who had suggested that I write a book. "Here it is," I said.

2. Winnicott (1947) states that the deeply regressed psychotic patient is not able to acknowledge his own hatred or to identify with the analyst any more than the newborn infant can sympathize with its mother. This, he points out, imposes an additional strain that the analyst needs to tolerate.

# Prologue

(Dr. Nakhla)

Grace walked into my office at our first meeting and, scarcely looking at me, handed me a letter from her former analyst, Dr. P., an old friend and colleague of mine. She had informed me in a phone call that she had just moved back to New York from London and had been referred to me by Dr. P. She had seemed eager to see me, and I looked forward to an interesting patient and a link with a fellow candidate from my psychoanalytic training. Dr. P.'s note was brief and personal, mentioning that she had seen Grace in psychotherapy for several months and that Grace was "intelligent, sensitive, talented, and insightful."

Grace was frail, thin, and boyish-looking and appeared timid and detached; she was soft-spoken and had a gentle expression and manner that gave away no feelings other

7

than a general discomfort. She seemed reluctant to discuss her problems or her previous treatment, and I found myself taking the initiative. Yet she somehow conveyed her anticipation that she would like to continue her therapy with me. I accepted this decision without further exploration, a reaction stemming in part from my desire to take over a treatment begun by a trusted colleague. We agreed to meet once a week, as she had done with Dr. P.

At our next meeting, Grace was silent. This silence was to continue for eighteen months. Grace will now tell her story and give some insight into the causes of her compelling need to be silent. Of course, I didn't get to know this story until much later in our work.

# 1
# Grace's Story

(Grace Jackson)

o

## A Perfect Child

I was always the oldest, as far back as I can remember. The feeling of being a child is taking care of: taking care of my mother, my sister Eleanor, fifteen months younger; keeping the family together. As though it all depended on me. I don't remember before Eleanor was born: as if we'd been born together. I remember waiting with Eleanor for our mother to come home from the hospital with Martha (I was almost four): someone else to take care of, though not in the same way as Eleanor and my mother— changing diapers, holding the bottle. Being the oldest means being good: being easy, helpful—one of my nicknames was Easy, another was Perfect. Being good also means being happy. Eleanor could get in a rage but I couldn't. We went to school very early; I was about two and a half. Eleanor always cried, but I liked going. I wanted everything to be neat and smooth, just as I insisted that my mother braid my hair every morning instead of merely running a comb through the front and tightening the barrettes.

I felt proud to be praised as good. It was the same at school: I was good or even the best at things. And once you start it's hard to stop: success encourages itself, while failure becomes more and more impossible to tolerate, or contemplate. I couldn't be bad or get a wrong answer; I couldn't even stand to be late for school. I would rush my sisters—and my mother—to get ready in the morning.

We appeared to be a happy family, to have a happy childhood, and in some ways we were, and did. No one talked about things beneath the surface. My room was next to my parents', and at night sometimes I would hear them fighting. It frightened me: I would imagine them going the next day to get a divorce. Many years later my mother said, "I don't remember that we fought at all." Or maybe what I envisioned as end-of-the-world battles was part of their relationship. Anyway, I thought that if I was good—that is, what I imagined my mother wanted—I would keep her happy and the family whole. I was terrorized—paralyzed—by the fear of her displeasure or disapproval. Someone once asked me if I had any memory of my mother praising me; and I didn't. What I remember is that she was always criticizing. Later I understood that she thought it was bad taste to praise one's children publicly. Yet this left me and my sisters not only vulnerable to criticism but suspicious—unaccepting—of praise.

My father was a less vivid presence, but in many ways I felt close to him, except, of course, when I thought he was the cause of my mother's displeasure or unhappiness. Like him, I loved maps and directions, trains and timetables, and going places.

Another part of growing up was the feeling of not being there: sometimes it was a literal feeling, sometimes it was the anxiety that I was not what I appeared to be, or would be unable to keep up the appearance, the person that had somehow emerged, that people called "Grace."

At fourteen I went away to boarding school, eager to get away from the familiar, the known, hoping that in a place where no one knew me I could start again, as if from the beginning, free of my old self: the good, the oldest, the best in school, the popular one. Free of what I was expected to be. Of course this didn't happen, and the first year was essentially a continuation of the past. The next year everything changed. Suddenly I was unhappy, I started doing badly in school, breaking rules; everything was a struggle for me, at school and at home. My parents understood this as "adolescence," a naturally difficult time, and didn't take my complaints very seriously. But to me the smallest thing seemed to matter intensely, I became obsessed with "meaning." In the summers of my second and third years of high school I worked as a counselor at a camp in Vermont. It was actually a farm, where there were animals and gardens to be tended, and buildings to be built. I loved it there; what you did made sense, was real: the garden had to be weeded, dinner had to be made. The director was starting a school on the same principles of "learning by doing" (history would be the history of the farm, science would be the weather and the ecology of the land), and on a visit in the fall of my last year of high school I decided I wanted to stay at the school. My parents insisted that I come home and discuss it. I stayed home for a week, and then went back to my old school. That was the most rebellious thing

I'd done in my life. In the end it was a disappointment; rather, I was a disappointment to myself.

In any case, I finished the year, and the next fall went to college. In a way it was a liberation. You could study pretty much what you wanted, do what you wanted. I started learning Greek, and read Dante for the first time. My Greek teacher was a man who had kept a diary for many years, and though he had written other things, he had come to see, he said, that the diary was his life's work. I had kept a diary since I was about twelve. In the beginning it was a daily record of what happened, what I did, what I felt, on the most basic, literal level. It was like a task that had to be done each day—not unenjoyable, but there was the page, with its date, needing to be filled up. Gradually it became more complex and introspective, and eventually the page came to represent me; in a sense, to be me: I could exist only if I was written down. It is the one solid, consistent thread in my life.

o

## Susan: A Mutual Attachment

My best friend in college was Susan. We were in the same freshman English class, we lived in neighboring dorms, we liked Pound, and early music. We read our poetry assignments out loud to each other and played recorders together. Superficially we were opposite: she appeared hard-edged, definite, she had opinions about everything, she seemed to know what she wanted and who she was, whereas I was very unsure of myself and what I wanted; I easily fitted in with whatever, whoever happened to be around. We wanted something in each other, from each other: I wanted her external aggressiveness, the ability to be angry, to argue, to know, and say, what she thought;

for her I represented a kind of gentleness, perhaps gener-
ousness, that was missing from her life. Of course this was
just the surface: her hardness concealed a deep insecurity,
my softness was turmoil. Like me, she kept a diary, and we
read our diaries to each other. We became attached. When
I read my diary, it—I—was being reflected in this other
person: I became a person through the act or fact of my
reading and her listening. Pretty quickly I felt lonely when
she wasn't around. One weekend at the end of the first year,
she went to New York with another friend, and didn't tell
me. I felt deserted, betrayed, and jealous. My mother, who
had met Susan a few times, at school and on a weekend
visit, didn't like her, and was pleased—she thought this
would detach us. I'd made the mistake of complaining to
her.

The second year we moved to the same dorm and had
next-door rooms at the end of a corridor. Every day after
breakfast we would walk out beyond the classroom buildings, past fields and a larch grove, to where the road ended
in another road. We would kick the rusted signpost, and
return to the day. We stayed up all night together, writing
papers, talking. No detail of life or books was too trivial to
be relentlessly examined. We weren't exclusive; Susan in
particular always had other friends—she liked to have a lot
of people around. I had friends, too, although often I felt
she didn't like them; I was afraid of her criticisms, her
disapproval. Even then people saw us as a sort of "couple,"
always together: the gold-dust twins, the college postmis-
tress called us.

From the start, there was also for me a kind of tension
having to do with being alone and being together. I always
wanted to have time alone; in that sense, I wanted Susan
to have other friends, particularly boyfriends, perhaps, as
they were not a real threat to our relationship. But I also
needed her to be present, so that I could see myself. We

imagined spending our lives together: two old ladies rocking on a front porch.

After college we decided to go to London. We both wanted to get away from our families, thinking that with distance and freedom we could separate from them and find ourselves. Susan wrote: "We love each other, we fascinate each other, we need each other, and fear each other. Our roles dance and jump around the rooms we have lived in, around the circles we have formed with our words and dreams."

In London we became more directly and intensely dependent on one another. For about three months we lived in a room at the YWCA across from the British Museum. We didn't know anyone, and we spent all our time together, a lot of it traveling to different neighborhoods looking for a flat. Finally we found a place, on the edge of Hampstead—one room, with a kitchen—and began to set up a household. We bought two plates, two forks, two cups. Susan got a job at a small publisher. I babysat, I worked at a women's center, I cleaned some houses, I walked all over North London. At night we would make dinner—Susan liked to cook; she found it relaxing after work—and tell each other about our days, as we had in college. We must have seemed very closed in, a world on our own. And I was not really interested in other people, did not think I needed them; nor did I understand the need that bound me in this relationship. Much later, when we were breaking up, Susan said that in the beginning our relationship was based on need: we simply needed each other.

We had come to London to find ourselves. My method was to go into myself, hers was to go into the world. College had had both an intellectual and a social structure; in London we had neither. The search for myself was between Susan and me. She was my connection to the alive world of people, events, activity—not only my connection but my viewpoint, my bond. This was how I wanted it. I was alone a lot and I wrote a lot: I described days in tremendous, excruciating detail (a conversation, the grocery shopping); often I went for long walks or bus rides, and afterward studied maps and bus routes to see where I had been, yet I never managed to reach myself. Sometimes I said to myself that I was practicing to be a writer, but that seemed as fraudulent, as unreal, as any of my other jobs. Solitude intensified such habits as being afraid of what people would think or say; a kind of shyness; awkwardness and self-consciousness. Besides, the English were not very outgoing or openly emotional: we really never did know what anyone thought. Yet while Susan found London uncongenial, I liked the unemotional English; I guess I found it safe. But I was also restless. We had already had some fights—she would get angry about my not saying what I felt or wanted in some situation or other, this being symptomatic to her, typical, of my whole way of being. She wanted me to be more independent, but I didn't see why it was necessary. But then I was very dependable for her: maybe that's what she needed. I guess she knew I wouldn't leave: I was the safe and dependable one.

I always wanted to be what Susan was—to have whatever she had: her job, her friends, her clothes, her women's group. Yet we enjoyed being with each other more than with anyone else; we liked our domestic life. After a year we moved to a bigger flat, near Hampstead Heath, and I started graduate school at London University, studying ancient languages. Our life seemed to have more shape. But that tentative shape turned out to be illusory; I didn't like school, after all, and eventually I decided to quit. I didn't know what I wanted to do. We had then been in London for about two years, and we decided to go back to America, to New York. There were practical reasons (Susan couldn't get a work permit, I was having a hard time finding a job), but mainly we felt that we could never feel really at home in England. We would always be outsiders, and uncomfortable, and therefore would never be, or find—or confront—our real, or true, selves there. So in September 1973 we were in New York, in an apartment Susan had found. I was glad to be in New York, and got a job as a proofreader right away: now I went out while Susan worked at home.

o

## First Analyst

Susan had started seeing an analyst, Dr. D., soon after we arrived in London, in an attempt to deal with her family problems. She urged me to see someone, too, because of my "repressing of emotions." In my family when we heard of someone going to a psychiatrist, we saw it as a sign of weakness, an admission that you couldn't solve your own problems. On the other hand, since I was alone so much, and spent so much time writing in my diary (by now I typed it), observing, recording, analyzing myself, I was interested to know about psychoanalysis. Every week when Susan came back from Dr. D.'s I wanted her to tell me about the session. And when I decided to see someone I thought of it not as seeking help but as a way to "know" myself. Through Dr. D. I went to Dr. P., whom I saw once a week for about eight months.

The first time I went to see her I answered her questions about my family, about what I was doing in London, but mostly I sat self-consciously twisting the buttons of my sweater and staring at the red Oriental rugs. The next week I twisted my hair and stared at the rugs till my eyes watered. "I talked and she talked and there were long awful silences; but something happened," I wrote in my diary. I was elated and depressed at once. What is your life in London like?

she asked. I talked about life at school and life at home, and their separateness, about old friends from America who were living in London—all the time thinking that what I was saying was superficial. There was a long silence. What are you thinking? she said. That I want to say something but don't know what or how. I told her how I can't talk when there is any sort of pressure: at school, or here, with her. But I write. "A diary? That is very good." And then I told her how I am unable to do what I really want, how I never feel involved: "There are always voices, forces that pull me from the center."

For example, she said (she often made up examples, stories): You meet someone, you want to see him or her again; you wait, he or she doesn't call as promised: what is your impulse? To call myself, I said. Yes, and why don't you? Fear that the person doesn't want to see me after all, and of appearing foolish. Do you remember anything in your childhood that could have caused you to feel this way? No, I said. It's been like this as long as I can remember. How old were you when Eleanor was born? Fifteen months. Of course you cannot remember that, but your mother, no matter how much she did not want to, must have neglected you somewhat for the new baby.

She elaborated: the monster is my relationship with Eleanor. I identified so closely with her that I could not believe she was a separate person: loving and hating, needing and fearing her, so that even now we hardly communicate. Writing and receiving letters, talking are too painful: there is nothing between us, for we are each other. When one is happy, the other is; when one suffers, so does the other. I saw her in a dream one night, walking up some stairs, and so beautiful I couldn't stand it. She is Medusa, the doctor said. If you look, you are turned to stone.

Medusa: that's what we used to call her, with her long wavy hair hanging snakelike around her head.

Extraordinary! she said. And to her you are Minerva, born from the head of the father, having no mother. Wise and powerful, but wearing helmet, armor, and shield, because she is in fact defenseless, vulnerable: she had no mother.

She quoted Dante: "Vergine Madre, figlia del tuo figlio." The child is mother to the mother.

A session in early June:

> I ramble and ramble between the silences. I laugh
> and say I am not making sense; I can't say what I
> want; what I mean or suppose I mean . . .* to say.
> The carpets have been cleaned; Dr. P. wears pale yel-
> low and white; smiles; is real . . . and then she fades.
> An image, a memory comes to mind. I talk, almost
> without thinking, hoping desperately for some sense,
> some meaning; hoping it will be the key, the sign.
>
> You are secretive.
>
> Yes I am intensely secretive. I am afraid. And I
> do not remember what it is that I am afraid of. A
> habit. Even when I think I am being open I am not.
> And whichever way I act, appear, whether open or
> consciously double-edged, I am sick afterward: it was
> no good. So they are merely different aspects of secre-
> tiveness; two different defenses; barriers between me
> and the outside. I felt shattered: not hysterical, just
> that I wanted quietly to collapse and cry.

Once when I was speaking of my fascination with maps and transportation, walking, and studying routes from place to place, she said, You always want to know where you are; and inside you never know where you are.

We talked about Susan: we must get to the root of this, she said. How did it begin? Where is it going, or is it static? There seems to be a fear of moving onward. Are you in love

* Ellipses used in the diary do not indicate omissions.

with her? she asked. I was startled. You have the same lack of freedom that comes of being in love; you lack the true freedom of loving. What she says makes sense. I would say that your relationship with Susan is what is called in loose terms "sick," she said. That is, your inability to leave each other, to make separate decisions. Are you afraid of Susan leaving you? Is she the replacement for Eleanor in the symbiotic relationship you seem to demand, to need? She pressed on: Why are you afraid to separate from Susan? You support each other's unreality. How real, then, is your relationship?

Sometimes, yes, it is unreal, and sometimes it seems like the only reality in the world. I tell her what we talk about here, she tells me what happens with Dr. D.; but I never tell her when we talk about her and me, because I am afraid that what I say to you is not the truth—is not any truth—but my own distorted version of the truth. And I began to cry: crying, and forgetting myself, until I remembered . . . I remembered Susan always saying how she cries, and fumbles for a kleenex, and the doctor sits unmoved. Thinking of that I looked up, and the doctor sat unmoved; so I just left the tears in my eyes.

I saw Dr. P. a last time, just before I left London. Susan was already gone. It was early September, after the summer vacation:

> The doctor: plump and sunburned, in a purple cotton dress. I stand waiting in her room, examining books, pictures, the view from the window into a green garden, a yellow-tiled terrace . . . I move from the window, to the blue and green Cézanne print, the framed plate of 19th-century women from a fashion magazine, the painted wood Virgin and Child hanging beside the door. The other end of the room, with its couches and chairs and coffee tables, seems a draw-

ing room. I think of Freud's Greek and Roman objects, of her saying she meets me as a person, herself: the room must be an expression of that person, and not sterile, soulless . . . She returns: Sit down. I was waking my father from his nap, she says. He is quite old, but should not sleep too long . . . I begin to tell her about Greece, my vacation; then we talk about America, about how I feel to be leaving England, returning home. And for the first time it was as if we really were two women meeting.

# 2
# A False Self

(October 1973–

March 1975)

○

## A Hidden Self

### (Dr. Nakhla)

At our second meeting Grace was silent. Little did I suspect that I would learn no more in the eighteen months to come. This silence in her weekly sessions was set against a blank, empty background; any exchanges we had were without spontaneity. Her body was noticeably still, and this unchanging picture was accentuated by her seeming to be dressed each week in the same nondescript clothes. She carried a large black bag, which she always placed in the same spot beside her chair; this bag, whose contents were a mystery, came to symbolize for me her world, the self that was kept hidden. She appeared each week, as if from nowhere, with disturbing punctuality, so that she never had to use the waiting room, and in time I found myself feeling controlled and irritated by this behavior, as though compelled to meet it with similar precision.

Many of my interventions were based on attempts to understand Grace's silence as resistance or transference manifestations. Periodically I would sit quietly with her in her silence, but this did not seem to be what she needed; rather, it seemed to make her more uncomfortable. At times, my sitting silently may have been generated more by my own stubbornness and anger, my sense of isolation and defensive detachment.

Grace always sat on the edge of her chair, her eyes downcast. She was able to tell me that she was terrified of being swallowed up and losing herself if she were to sit back in the deep chair. In spite of this, I sometimes found myself responding to her detached stillness and her silence as though she were communicating a simple absence of feelings and thoughts. I would comment or, at exasperated moments, get into one-sided arguments about the impossibility of her mind being totally blank, and would prod her to talk. On one occasion, I sat beside her and suggested that we play a game of ticktacktoe; another time I got her to pound her fist on the arm of the chair. She readily complied, but nothing else emerged.

In retrospect, I can see that my questions and interpretations were attempts to impose meaning on Grace's mental state and behavior, attempts that were derived from psychoanalytic formulations relevant to a person with less profoundly disturbed psychic functioning. Other interventions and direct manipulations were clumsy attempts to bring about a change in her behavior and were blatant expressions of countertransference reactions to Grace's terrifying

sense of inner deadness and nonexistence and to the absence of meaningful contact between us. I was coping with
the disquieting awareness that my sense of myself as a
human being and my role as a psychoanalyst were contin-
ually being obliterated. Even my starting the sessions on
time—an experience that carries meaning in the analytic
interaction—had no significance and became merely an au-
tomatic action that I had to perform.

Grace did allow me to know of the importance of her
diary writing. Through pages of her diary that she gave me
to read and through her letters (Dr. P. had confidentially
sent me a copy of a letter Grace had written to her early in
her treatment with me), I came to recognize her feelings of
unreality and futility and her suicidal thoughts. I struggled
to conceptualize her psychic state, yet it seemed beyond
my grasp. My hope of reaching her through her diary also
came to nothing. I found the pages she gave me cumber-
some to read: a cataloguing of thoughts, perceptions, and
states of mind that did not touch me. I also felt shut out by
the pages themselves, solid with single-space type, with
narrow margins and no paragraph breaks. At one point I
remarked that there was a boring deadness in what she
wrote. I realized later that she experienced this comment, which was perhaps accurate and also central to her
anxieties, as a mortifying rejection; it may also have accounted for her showing me very little of her diary during
this time.

Clearly I contributed to the impasse over these months
of a treatment that in essence never came to life. I
managed to sustain my interest and curiosity, however,
and, although frustrated and puzzled, I continued to
be there. Grace "watched and waited" (as she put it in
one of her diary pages), holding on to a distant and dim
hope.

o

## A Hopeless Struggle

### (Grace Jackson)

I went to see Dr. Nakhla for the first time in October 1973. I had dreamed of being taken to my new psychiatrist by my old one. What is your problem? he said. I didn't know how to answer. He went on asking questions, about England, about my family, about Susan: I felt that he was just trying to find something I would talk about— anything—but I couldn't respond. I was nervous and afraid of him; what I did say seemed superficial, didn't ring true. When I left, I felt sick to my stomach. With Dr. P. I had felt some sort of connection and sympathy, whereas this doctor was strange, distant, except in his being connected to her, an extension of her: "Dr. P. knows both of us, and if she thinks this would be a good relationship perhaps we ought to trust her," I wrote in my diary, describing the conversation.

The first difficulty—perhaps symbolic—was the office: I hated it, especially after Dr. P.'s office, which was a room in her house, a long room running from front to back on the second floor of a North London row house. There was a daybed with a blanket folded at the foot, there were the Oriental rugs, there were the pictures, and objects. The room was light, and through the window you could see the top of a tree in the garden, the backs of other houses. Sterile, impersonal, formal were the words I used in my diary to describe my new doctor's office, which was in a ground-floor apartment shared by several doctors, with a common waiting room. The rooms were dark, so that even when it was light outside the lamps were lit. His room had a green carpet, gold-patterned walls, matching armchairs in front of a fireplace, with a glass-topped table between them. On

the table were two matching heavy glass ashtrays. Against
the wall as you came in was a bookcase, containing only
psychiatric books. I wrote to Dr. P. after I had been seeing
Dr. Nakhla for about two months:

> I have been going to see Dr. Nakhla and mostly we
> have been talking (or not talking) about why I cannot
> talk to him; why even when I say something it com-
> municates nothing. An old pattern; but relived each
> week with such intensity that when I leave I think
> my head will split and I don't want anything to do
> with any person in the world. I don't know how I feel
> about him; when I am there I mostly feel terrible, as if
> I am involved in a hopeless struggle; but the hope-
> lessness is real and true as almost nothing else is: in
> that sense it is good—I guess I believe somehow that
> it is not infinite or I would just have to kill myself,
> metaphorically or otherwise.

I went on in the letter, describing my life in New York:

> The days have become well-patterned; I make my
> way easily through them. When I stop to look at my-
> self, with thousands of other commuters, sitting all
> day in the office, clearing my desk at 5 to go home, I
> am surprised at the ease, the familiarity with which I
> deal with everything; it gives me a sense of accom-
> plishment, but it's unreal, it doesn't mean anything; I
> am untouched. I am seeing that I can survive the
> world, and that, I guess, is a necessity, but between
> that and me is an awful space.

I was afraid to say anything in the doctor's office because what I said might not be the truth. I had come to
New York to discover the truth: I was going to become
myself. I wanted to be able to talk without worrying about

what the other person might be thinking: but I wanted to be sure that what I said was really what I wanted to say. The first year nothing much happened; from the first session I sat on the edge of the chair and didn't say anything. But in the doctor's office you are supposed to talk; and when he asked questions I would make an effort to answer, though my answers often sounded false: struck a false note, my voice seeming to be not my voice. Usually I felt that I had failed: I had not been able to present the absolute truth from my point of view; my observing self was always critical, always adjusting the words, and never satisfied. But also I had not given the "right" answer or response from his point of view. In spite of myself I was afraid of what he thought: I often thought that he wasn't listening, wasn't paying attention to me, and that he didn't remember what I said—didn't remember me—from one time to the next. And that intensified the feeling of not saying the right thing, the truth. (Once he gave me the wrong bill: it confirmed my fear.) So I sat, nervous and stiff, on the edge of the chair by the window, and tried to respond to the doctor's gestures (we play ticktacktoe; he gets me to bang my fist on the arm of the chair; he tells me to lie on the couch, sit in the other chair, stand at the window and talk about the street outside); and his questions: Do you read a lot . . . What do you read . . . What are you feeling . . . Did you play as a child . . . How does the chair feel . . . Is it uncomfortable, how is it uncomfortable . . . And your clothes, do you ever wear anything different? (Once he told me to take the forty dollars for the session and buy something to wear.) . . . Do you think about Dr. P.? What was it like? Why was it different?

"I am just trying to find out what *is* real to you," he said. "I talk too much; out of proportion. I am supposed to listen. I ask questions that you hardly answer—I don't care what you talk about, I'm not trying for any specific thing, I

just want you to talk. In the end what I feel is that although
you come here to me, I must somehow come to you."

In my diary I wrote:

> I am sick of repeating my conversations with the
> doctor; the words are always the same. Maybe I will
> break down, break out, lose control. Or maybe I will
> just go on, sleepwalking, daydreaming, in that futile
> lifeless paralyzing gap between the serene face with
> its depths of mysterious calm and the screaming rag-
> ing violence. Not anger but destruction he called it.
> He talks and talks, to me, at me; on the edge of the
> chair, looking at nothing, I curl, I coil, tighter and
> tighter; it all has to do with someone else, someone I
> don't recognize, yet who is at the same time horribly
> well known.

> He asks questions but I feel that he isn't inter-
> ested in the answers. The feeling that I don't matter,
> that he is doing a job, as boring to him as my job is to
> me, pretending a sort of interest as I do with commas,
> or the alignment of the folio with the type. This one
> mean little hour: it's just another fantasy. Another
> grasping at a pretense for existence.

I almost never talked about my actual life, because I
felt that I didn't exist in it, or anywhere, except perhaps in
my diary. On the surface I did have a life: I was good at my
job, I was involved in office life, I had made friends there
and outside:

> I think of reality as having no connection to events, to
> the forms and activities of a life; at the same time it is
> contained in the smallest details. The arrangement of
> books on the table, a smell in the kitchen, the orange
> glare of the streetlight through the bedroom window

. . . I cannot talk about my life; there is nothing to tell. I went to work; Neil came to dinner, Lynn came to dinner. I made paella with the fish that Eyre gave me; I washed the dishes . . . Judy's nose was bitten in the park by a Doberman; Becky spent the day fuming behind a closed door; Margaret says, Those words look as if they should be capped. There is no consistency, no wholeness; only fragments.

In a letter to the doctor during his summer vacation in August 1974, after I had been seeing him for nearly a year, I wrote:

I truly do not believe that I am real. I am a shadow. It shocks me when someone says "I like you"—what is there to like or dislike in a shadow, a nonexistence. Even a fact becomes converted to fantasy, another fabrication, another dream, a nightmare . . . There is no separation of real and unreal, internal and external, no conflict, as I always thought: for nothing is allowed existence, allowed birth into the world. I feel naked; some form called Grace takes up space, but even that form is an illusion, a chameleon-like thing, taking on the colors of its surroundings . . . And so even this letter disgusts me, the detachment from what I am saying, the *form* of it. I hate both what is said and the I who says it. No wonder I never talk.

If I had been telling the truth of myself, I thought, it would have been reflected in him. The most vivid experience of this was when I gave him some pages of my diary to read. I had always thought that in my diary I said things more clearly—more truthfully—than I ever could talking: in terms not only of expression but of feeling:

The purple clouds that cling around the street lamps enlarge as the light turns from day to night; the sky

has a bright blue moment (even though it has been
gray all day) before blackness. City blackness is never
quite black anyway; not like the country, where on a
moonless, starless night sky, earth, air fuse in an im-
penetrable black. Groping. No, it's different in the
city: in various (and sundry, as they say) cities I have
known. Lights: streetlights, headlights, neon, isolated
lights in rooms: all, the sky reflects, refracts, distorts,
swallows: adulterating its blackness . . . I think I must
have strayed: I didn't mean to go outside, but then it's
as well to know where you stand; for you to know
where I stand. More accurately, where I sit, for I am
sitting, in a cane-seated chair at a light-wood table
whose varnish is peeling in gray streaks. My walls are
white; there is a light hanging from the ceiling, just
over my right eye; the light hangs yellow, a yellow
circle over the table spreading onto the floor. The
floors of this apartment are wood, parquet. My picture
of the street is slatted by venetian blinds: my vision
of the world outside (world? outside?). Back to the
External; I wanted to say what it was; it should be
clear, separated as it is by those slats. Room/Street.
Prisonlike; only bars, I think, are mostly vertical. It
should be clear; but like those boxes children draw,
when you do not know if you are looking left to right
or right to left, out to in or in to out, I do not know if
I am inside looking out or outside looking in, or even
if I can use those words, which themselves imply distinction. And my dreams: the boundary of waking
and sleep is blurred; people, places, conversations,
even feelings: I do not know if they have been fabri-
cated by life or by sleep. Either way they're a fabrication, and so why bother with definition . . . I ate a fig,
an old dry fig, and meanwhile the sky has disappeared.

Enough: I am not getting any closer. The page is a
long time filling. And a woman's life is measured in
pages filled: full pages, the print crowded, the margins slim. Double spaces, two-inch margins—cheat-
ing. A strange life, which can only be accounted in
black and white: black and yellow, in fact, which is a
little degrading. She can't seem to get off the page;
trembling she clutches. If she moves she might see
herself and then there would be no solution but the
razor blade. What a leap! Cold and friendless in her
silent house she hovers, barren blind.

A woman, thin and tired, watches the rain; has
watched the rain through many windows, felt the rain
in the streets and meadows, on mountains and the
decks of ships; November rain, March rain, August
rain, rain that chills and rain that refreshes; rain that
kills and rain that rejoices. She dreams now into the
rain, backward into the past, past rains, rains of the
past, her past. The voice of rain on a tin roof; the
burst of rain from an African cloud that passes as
quickly as it marred the brilliant sky; raindrops clinging to the grasses of a Vermont meadow, the red-
skinned brambles; the streaming wind-blown rain that
lashes windowpanes, gashes and reddens the cheeks
of a girl running over the treeless top of Parliament
Hill; the fine streaming rain that soaks through
clothes to the skin (she is lying on the open deck of a
ship, watching the dawn-gray cliffs of England near);
running naked through a sloping tree-ringed field;
merely watching, the puncturing of puddles, their
shine, the sparkle of thin branches, speckling of glass,
umbrellas held high in defense. So much rain; every
drop a story, all boring, as bored as endless watching,
endless waiting. Always she is watching, always wait-

ing. Part of the dream: a dream spun out to nothing, to the varying rhythms of rain. She cannot transcend the woman-in-the-room; yet the image grows stale; grows hollow; and remains, superposed, large, threatening. She, the image, must be smashed; but who will pick up the pieces? Sweep them under the couch or behind the door? (It doesn't matter, as long as they are out of sight.) There is music, trumpets, to absorb the sound, but blood and guts make quite a mess, you would imagine, having never literally seen.

After he read those pages he said yes, they were written well, even beautifully, but they were dead. That was his idea about me, I thought, and he was fitting into that idea whatever—what little—I gave him. It was not until years later that he came to understand what I was trying to express: the first passage was, as he put it, an attempt to find myself in the dimension of space (geography); the second an attempt to find myself in the dimension of time (memory, history).

o

## Susan: Breaking Away and a Breakdown

### (Grace Jackson)

Susan and I were starting to come apart. Instead of lessening, the tensions that had appeared in London increased. I suppose we were feeling trapped by each other. I wrote in my diary: "She is depressed, and mostly alone; I can't stand that; and am always thinking there is something I am doing or not doing; that my very existence depresses her." I often felt violently angry; I began to resent and to be jealous of her other friends. I felt wildly inferior, ignored, abandoned: yet at the same time I wanted to be free of her, I wanted to be alone. I walked and I wrote. I was restless. In London we had had a real household, with rituals, habits; it was almost an extension of college in the way we shared everything. In New York this changed: our daily lives were more separate; we didn't spend as much time together. And every once in a while we would have a terrible fight:

> Her old complaint, differently expressed, a variation: I do not talk to her, don't say when I'm angry or annoyed. She feels my self-destructions as a sign of hatred, of anger against her. I sit unspeaking, unmoving, she furious at my blankness, and I wanting to burst with it. I don't believe you don't feel anything: what do you fill your pages with? she goads me, like the doctor. And then I do burst: I am always wanting to be you, and at the same time struggling to be independent. The boundary between us is vague for me; everything I do or even think is in terms of you, or you-and-me, but never me alone . . . She: I guess I sort of know that; and I hate being in that position. And I know that, and hate myself for it.

In the spring of 1974 Susan began having anxiety attacks whenever she went outside. She was having a nervous breakdown, she said: "It's something I have to go through. A physical nervous breakdown." According to the arrangement of our relationship I was now supposed to stay strong. "She has immense power over me," I wrote. "She would say she wants not to have it, but she does; she somehow needs it." When she had to go somewhere I had to take her.

> Susan calls: she is with Alix [a friend], will sleep there. I am alone, deserted. There are all my emotions: that is what I have never discussed with the

doctor. What truly dominates my life . . . And so I
launch into one of my exaggerated hurts. Not exaggerated, given that what I want from her, from our relationship, is some kind of total self-containment . . . In
the light of day I see my foolishness, the unreality I
create, the impossibility; when she doesn't talk to me
I am paralyzed. Enslavement. I can't be separate. She
has a headache; she can't go out alone; walking she
gets dizzy, as if to faint. What does that mean? It
makes me so afraid I can't stand it.

There was a kind of respite in the fall of 1974, when I
changed jobs and went to work as an assistant to a writer
at a magazine. When I was interviewed, he asked, "Are you
a stable person?" I reassured him: I can do anything. That
was it: I felt that no matter how distressed or chaotic I
might be inside I would always be able to keep up appear-
ances outside; it was what I had been doing for all of my
life. Between jobs I went to Oregon to visit my sister Eleanor
for a week. When I got back, the doctor said I seemed
different, more "there"; and I sat back a little in the chair.

At the same time, Susan had started seeing Larry
(whom she eventually married), and it became increasingly
clear what was going to happen. In a sense I had always
wished that she would find a boyfriend—always wished
that a relationship would work out—so that I would be able
to be alone: free was how I thought of it. But when it
actually happened what I saw was how dependent I was,
or had been, and what I felt was that I would never exist
on my own. I became more and more isolated and cut off,
from both friends and my family; the person I wanted to
be with did not have time for me. Yet I was still unable to
talk to the doctor, even to tell him what was happening.
Susan not only spent most of her time with Larry, she

ignored me; and the more she ignored me the more I seemed to need her. I think she had to, in order to break away—while I became more clinging, not outwardly but in feeling more and more acutely the lack of a self.

I spent days and nights writing, trying to analyze what was happening, and always ending in despair. I wished my body would disappear: I walked to get rid of my restlessness, I was hardly able to eat, I slept in a sleeping bag on the floor in the living room, and a frequent image was of flattening my body into it. I was overwhelmed, I seemed to be breaking into pieces, my body felt sick, my mind felt sick, I was destructive and destroyed.

> I want to be stripped to a skeleton, in order to feel the presence, the physical existence of my body. No fat, no flesh between it and feeling. Similarly the mind. This stripping makes me easily hurt, so exposed, everything is painful.
>
> And thus you know that you exist; that you have not disappeared. Like scraping your hand along a brick wall to see the blood: you see the blood, you know that you are real.
>
> But then I think I am making it up, fabricating the pain, or at least the cause of it; I should not be feeling it, and I don't understand why I do: and suddenly even the pain is unreal, as unreal as the surface, the facade.

We had to make a decision about the actual living situation: what made sense—perhaps because I was so extreme in my desire not to appear hurt—was for me to move out and for Larry to move in. Somehow I managed to find an apartment, but before I moved I helped with his moving: this was the most disturbed but most poignant moment of all. It was as though I were pushing myself out of my house, active in my own destruction, while it might simply have seemed that I was being a good friend. "Brave," said Susan.

> It is not my house anymore; I am visiting among the plants and the dark heavy furniture . . . The floor is cleared, but the closets are bulging. Even my bedroom, the alcove, is lined with Larry's records; couch, chair, tables, wooden trunk; an old Pepsi machine he bought for $5 . . . In the bedroom a double bed and furniture piled around it. I am dispossessed, displaced. My presence is no more in this house. A strange awful feeling. Where are the spaces, the bareness? My house will be bare; this is like a real house, a home; I am afraid of my own emptiness. Emptiness of my house . . . Nightmare days and nights, being pushed out of my house. There just is not room.

At the same time I became more frightened of being alone: I imagined that I would go into my apartment, close the door, and die. The doctor's office was the only safe place, where I could be contained and, at least for that hour, would not disappear. I cried and cried in the doctor's office. And he suggested that I go to the hospital: as a place to cry, a rest. I said, I'll do whatever you say. Perhaps I would figure out how to live by myself—without Susan.

# 3
# First
# Hospitalization

(March 1975)

o

## A False Calm

### (Grace Jackson)

I spent most of my time in the hospital trying to understand what I was doing there. I was disturbed, distressed, upset, both physically and mentally: confused. I didn't know what to do with myself, or what I was doing: in the hospital, in my life. This stay in the hospital was an extension of my life, in the sense that I was still aware of myself, still watching myself: as in (from the hospital record) "Pt [patient] superficial about problems"; as in the distance between descriptions of the patient in the nurses' reports and what she writes in her diary. And maybe the distance was not as great as in the regular outside world,

where I had continued to work and even to see people;
where I had dealt with the reality of Susan and Larry, of
finding an apartment, signing the lease, while feeling in
pieces inside. You might imagine that in the hospital this
barrier between inside and outside would break down; I
wished that it would, that I would be literally out of my
mind. But I didn't ever really stop thinking, or trying, as I
said, to figure out. I never rested from my mind, or got any
rest from it: where am I, what am I doing here, what does
it mean, how does it feel? Or, for another example, I felt
guilty that Susan had to take care of business-type things
for me and that only she knew where I was. (After two or
three days I told my sister Martha, and then my parents; at
that time I didn't want—I refused—to see my parents, although eventually I did. They came to see me.) Besides, in
the hospital the goal is to make you able to deal with the
world, so that's what doctors, nurses, therapists of many
kinds were trying to do.

In the doctors' and nurses' notes there is a great emphasis on appearance and eating: "Pt didn't eat well . . .
Not well groomed, wearing same clothes . . . seclusive;
remained in room . . ." I cried a lot, I was depressed and
bored: but partly that had to do with the place itself. And
in the end I went along with it, complied as I had in all
other aspects, all other periods of my life. ("Neatly
dressed," say the notes. "Pleasant appearance . . . Socialized
in dayroom, joined activities. Watched TV, played Scrabble.") I began to take it as an experience in itself, with its
own interest. I read; sat on the windowsill looking out at
unfamiliar Brooklyn; smoked cigarettes in the dayroom;
took part in activities. There was a relentless cheerfulness,
in spite of, for example, the boy, Kevin, with heavily bandaged wrists; or those who with dazed or glazed expressions shuffled endlessly up and down, up and down the
orange-carpeted hall. How are you today? the nurses say

brightly, coming on duty. But everyone was in some way damaged, of course. You were supposed to "relate" to the others, socialize, though there wasn't much in common— not even (or maybe in particular) the reason for being there. My roommate was a depressed old woman who snored. The very idea of roommates seemed counterproductive; and yet you were supposed to "get along."

On the other hand, the hospital was a container at a time when I needed to be contained, when perhaps the doctor also needed me to be contained; maybe he thought it would calm me down—that is, that I would be able to cry as long as I needed to without worrying about daily life, and then would be able to go to my apartment without thinking I was going to die. And some things touched me. I felt that I had some relationship with Dr. S., the resident in charge of me, even though I don't think he really understood what I was going through. There was the body experience of yoga; also the experience of making pots. Finally, there was one occupational therapist, Bob, whom I think I liked: he told me about the Quaker cemetery in Prospect Park, in Brooklyn: on a hill, hidden, in the middle. I had never been to Prospect Park; maybe I felt something hopeful about this. After the first week, I went out for a day, to my apartment. After the second week (I was to leave at the end of the third week) I had a weekend pass to move. My father came to help me, and a friend who lived in the neighborhood; Susan was there, too. Later I wrote about dividing everything up—the books, the dishes—but then I didn't care, I just wanted it to be done.

In another way, maybe hopelessness was a feature of the hospital: the quick-fix, band-aid approach, which I felt was essentially useless, as though I knew what was going to happen in the next months, after I left and did go into that apartment: when you might say the real breakdown began. The final doctor's report from the hospital says,

"Patient well dressed, neatly dressed—improved affect and sociability . . ." and "Improvement definitely shown."

o

## A Change of Approach

**(Dr. Nakhla)**

Grace had gone through the breakup of her life with Susan alone, without being able to tell me about her anguish until the very end. She came to a session at that point sobbing, feeling depersonalized—"My head does not feel attached to the rest of my body"—and terrified that she was going to die. This jolted me into an anxious state. I was certainly unprepared, and I dealt with my confusion and the threat that Grace was experiencing a psychotic decompensation and was possibly suicidal by deciding to place her in the hospital. (Apparently, I vented my feelings by almost shouting at her. From Grace's diary: "You have been feeling all this and you can't even tell your bloody psychiatrist!") I suggested to Grace that the hospital was a place where she could let go of her feelings and express them.

For three weeks, Grace was at Brookdale Hospital, where I was director of psychiatric residency training. I visited her regularly but chose not to participate actively in her treatment; I welcomed the opportunity to get the hospital staff's view of her condition. In fact, her hospitalization was remarkably uneventful, and she made a quick "recovery." She was given a diagnosis of depression and placed on an antidepressant medication.

Grace's hospitalization permitted me to step back and take a fresh look at what had gone on between us over the previous eighteen months. As I read her letters and diary pages again, I was struck by her acute sense of nonexistence and her feelings of unreality and futility toward what she experienced as her false self and her false life. I now recognized that these feelings had been clearly expressed in her writing and that I had been unable to relate to them.

In pursuing my new path toward understanding Grace's psychic state, I turned to Winnicott, specifically to his paper "Ego Distortions in Terms of True and False Self" (1960c), and to Deutsch's (1942) classic paper that presented the first clinical studies of what she termed the "as-if" personality. Winnicott developed his concept of true and false self in a number of papers (1949a, 1955, 1960c, 1963b). Laing, in his first book, "The Divided Self" (1960), gives a rich existential study with succinct phenomenological accounts of the experience of self-alienation. He uses the terms "death-in-life," "unembodied self," and "false self" to describe the sense of not being oneself.

I was familiar with these ideas. During my psychoanalytic training, in London in the mid-1960s, one of my control cases fell into the category of what Winnicott would term an analysis done on the basis of work with the false self. My experience with this analysand also seemed to fit closely Deutsch's description of one of her cases of an as-if personality: "The analysis was extremely rich in material but progressed in an emotional vacuum. While the transference was frequently represented in his [the patient's] dreams and fantasies, it never became a conscious emotional experience" (p. 274). In my control case, the analysand did not complain of the impoverishment or absence of his emotions, and it became apparent only after almost two years of analysis. In an attempt to work with his lack of feelings, I suggested that he sit in the chair and face me. His first remarks to me were perplexing and most unsettling: "I know I have been coming here five times a week for two years and lying on this couch. If you were to tell me that it never happened I could believe you. That's the way it feels." (Winnicott's ideas of the true and false self split were discussed in supervision, but my emigration to the United States precluded any further analytic work in this case.)

In contrast, as Deutsch points out, the clinical picture can take another form; as in Grace's case, the patient may be acutely aware of and distressed by the emotional defect. In Grace's letter to Dr. P. at the beginning of our treatment, she describes the experience of her silent sessions as a "hopeless struggle; but the hopelessness is real and true as almost nothing else is: in that sense it is good." On the other hand, of her accomplished and very effective false self, which carried her smoothly through her daily activities, she says, "It's unreal, it doesn't mean anything; I am untouched . . . and between that and me is an awful space."

Also, in her letter to me a year after the treatment began, she explicitly states that she does not believe she is real and describes her inner experience of her self as "a shadow," "a nonexistence," "a form called Grace that takes up space," "an illusion," "a chameleonlike thing, taking on the colors of its surroundings." I would now say that these descriptions indicate an extreme degree of dissociation, suggesting a failure of the earliest development of personalization, the sense of a body self.

Winnicott (1960c), in discussing the consequences of the concepts of true and false self for the clinical practice of psychoanalysis, writes:

> A principle might be enunciated, that in the False
> Self area of our analytic practice we find we make
> more headway by recognition of the patient's non-
> existence than by a long-continued working with the
> patient on the basis of ego-defence mechanisms. The
> patient's False Self can collaborate indefinitely with

the analyst in the analysis of defences, being so to
speak on the analyst's side of the game. This unre-
warding work is only cut short profitably when the
analyst can point to and specify an absence of some
essential feature: "You have no mouth," "You have
not started to exist yet," "Physically you are a man
but you do not know from experience about mascu-
linity," and so on. These recognitions of important
fact, made clear at the right moments, pave the way
for communication with the True Self. (1965, p. 152)

Heeding Winnicott's principle, I decided to change my
approach, and direct my attention toward recognizing and
attempting to reach Grace's true self. To accomplish this
more intensive analytic work, I suggested to Grace that after
her discharge from the hospital we increase our sessions to
four times a week. I also recommended a weekly session
with her parents. I had had experience as a family therapist,
and I reasoned that I could use the family structure to work
with Grace in her vulnerable and isolated state. She went
along with these proposed changes without any questions.

# 4
# A Violent Delusional State

(April–

November 1975)

○

## Life Feelings: Intolerable Destruction

**(Grace Jackson)**

I came from the hospital to an apartment I recognized only by its furnishings, its things: the chair, the rug, the dresser, the books, the baskets hanging on the wall. I could see they were mine; but I did not see myself. I had a little hope: that it would become familiar, that I would find myself in it. I wrote: "As long as I can see the doctor I think I can manage . . . manage? What does that mean? I will not fall to pieces. Really? Well, I am not at all sure." And: "I have been away for 3 weeks and I cannot say where I have been. Sick. Very sick. Yes I'm better now. A blatant lie: I am not at all better; it seems sometimes that I have

simply postponed the collapse; slowed it down." All my
life I had been saying everything was fine, when I knew it
wasn't; now I had had the chance to say so out loud and
be listened to, but it wasn't very loud and I wasn't sure if
I'd been heard, or if I believed it myself.

The first setback was that I lost my job: the writer I
worked for found out that I had been in a psychiatric hospital and did not want me to work for him anymore. Instead
of telling me himself he called the doctor, who then told
me. I was sent to work in another department of the magazine, but for two hours a day I did typing for the writer. I
was angry and humiliated; and it was a surprise to see that
what I thought of as my inner, private self could have an
effect on my external self-in-the-world.

I now saw the doctor four times a week; on one of those
nights, after my session, there was a family session with
my parents. I hated this, but I agreed because the doctor
said it was necessary. A session at the end of April, described in my diary (from the time I first started seeing the
doctor, I had tried to record some version of every session:
fragments, impressions, whole dialogues . . . ):

> I pace the doctor's office, animal in a cage, shred-
> ding kleenex, dropping it on the floor. To the corner,
> break off a piece of the potted plant in the corner, it
> is dry and brittle, crumble it, throw it at the chair, at
> the doctor.
>
> My parents, I talk to them now, too, but again it
> is meaningless. Friends too. There's nothing wrong
> with you: you speak so well about how you feel, what
> you think: you must be all right.
>
> What do any of you know?
>
> I paced, and threw the crumbled leaf over his
> clean shiny suit. I was acting, moving, expressing de-
> structiveness. And as long as it is confined (oh what a

word) to crumbling leaves and shredding kleenexes,
everyone is safe. But there is no guarantee that it will
be confined; it could break out any time: I could
break. I know that and am afraid. But yesterday in
spite of that rational fear I bought a package of razor
blades.

I would usually walk to work; walk during my lunch
hour; walk home. At home I would make up ways to get
myself through the evening: "Point to point: at 10:30 watch
Monty Python; 12:30, yoga; cigarette; something to eat;
sweep the floor." I did a few things like building bookshelves with bricks and boards, scraping paint off windowpanes. I hemmed a skirt, watched movies on TV.

And yet I am frightened. I hate this room because
it is my house and how has it come about that I have
a house, a place to come home, to sleep in, eat in.
Why couldn't I go on working, move to the new
house, go out, invite people over, go once or twice a
week to my psychiatrist to probe the past? Why can't
I spend a day with Emily, an evening with Christo-
pher, go home, perhaps read for a while, and then go
to sleep? Why must I take a sleeping pill or spend
hours working the nausea out of me?

The doctor: he takes my hand, puts his arm
around me, hand on my head. Then I am there, he is
there: real. Physical. But I go out into the vacuum of
the streets. Sun, wind, walkers, shoppers. I join them;
they perceive nothing wrong, or nothing at all. What
do other people do with their rage, their violence,
their destructiveness? Sitting with the doctor I want
to kill myself; end myself, fall away, out of sight forever. I can't sustain what I feel, can't endure it; and
yet I can no longer deny it, no longer put away onto

this or that event or experience, experience of past or
present, person of past or present: dark harvest of the
past. It is all stuck inside me, festering, gangrenous.
In old days they would have bled me with leeches,
stuck the slimy sucking things over my body to draw
out the bad blood, leaving me whole and healthy. I
might have died in the process, but it was the only
cure they knew. I want to leech myself, the sharp new
double-edged blades, but I might die in the process;
and though I see no way of living, I do not think
really that I want to die.

I do as I am told: go to the doctor, go to work,
because I have been told that I am going to get better;
and in the middle of the day, roaming the lunch-hour
streets, I wonder; and I come home and I wonder.

I thought about death; wrote about it, wrote it: my
death. I imagined I was writing suicide notes to all my
friends, whom more and more I didn't want to see. Feelings
became focused in my body, the physical. "Not sleeping,
as well as being a way of controlling the body, trying to
make it disappear, is also a way of making it feel. Making
it defenseless and weak; I *feel* the ache of my legs, of my
back; heaviness of my eyes." I thought about the razor
blades. But first I cut my hair. "Mutilation" I called it, and
imagined my mother crying, What have you done to yourself?

I used to have it long, hanging in my face, covering
my face; and now my face is naked, open to the
world, standing alone and empty. Empty: perhaps
that is the word, the definition.

I sat in the middle of my floor shredding newspapers. The
whole Sunday Times. Then I put the pieces into a bag to

throw away, except for one bouquet, which I put into a pot I had made, to give to the doctor. Only days after I had done it—the pot with its bouquet sat on my table—did I see that it was myself holding the pieces of myself. I brought it to the doctor:

> Bouquet of newspapers in a blue and black glazed pitcher. He pulled out the newspapers, threw them on the floor. That really is you. I pick up the paper from the floor, tear it into smaller and smaller pieces. Yes, I'm giving the pot to you, I made it myself. I think I will take it home and put flowers, not newspaper in it, he says. I am holding on to him: what can you do with these shreds? Newspaper all over us. That's how you feel. Uncontained by the pot, the shiny surface. You know, I don't really like that pot; it reminds me of the empty you. I look questioningly at him: can I? He nods, yes, and I throw it. I never thought I could destroy anything I made; I could be careless but never deliberately, consciously destroy. It gives a kind of hope that I can destroy the unliving, self-containing part of myself; but at the same time is the fear that having once begun I will be unable to stop destroying.

I tried to keep my house clean, the dishes washed, the roaches under control. But then it would deteriorate: there would be dust thick on the surfaces, newspaper fragments in the rug, bags of garbage that I couldn't manage to take out, litter, clutter, bugs. I tried also to stay in touch with the people I knew: to have lunch, or drinks, or go to the movies. In the very beginning both the doctor and my parents also tried to push me. But it became more and more difficult, more and more I hated it, wanted to be alone, and isolated.

My body is so weak . . . and then comes a burst of
energy, and I don't know what to do with it. Only
pour it into meaningless pages: when I return from
anywhere, anyone, anything, I must vomit it out. This
writing is not completion, fulfillment, crystallization
of experience, as I used to think, but getting rid of
anything that has touched me.

I kept tearing up newspapers in the middle of the night;
my apartment—a room, really—faced a small courtyard
with an ailanthus tree. I wore a hospital gown that somehow I had kept. I wrote: I would start out describing, and
end in a frenzy. I was now taking Libriums: I was supposed
to think of them as the good doctor; sometimes it worked.
Only with the doctor did I feel any sense of, or being in
touch with, myself; and it vanished as soon as I went out
the door, and the next time had to be achieved all over
again. "The awkwardness, then words, then word-sickness,
then maybe tears," for the hundredth, the millionth time.
    I started collecting glass: pieces of bottles, fragments.
But I started cutting with razor blades, scratching at my
wrists. As the marks disappeared, I felt I had to make new
ones, "to keep myself alive."

The doctor says You are afraid to break down because you think I cannot take it: I am in the chair
crying, crying to myself, my head is aching, crying to
myself, holding myself. Holding myself against the
moment of leaving. But I am also afraid that if I really
broke down I would not be able to leave . . . And in
between you are filled with anger toward me, you kill
and destroy me again and again . . . The moment I
walk out the door it begins . . . Oh hold my head;
stop the splitting ache. For a moment it works; I feel
him; I am me; just being. And then it becomes nulli-

fied, falsified, like everything else. I do not want to go
out there and start lying again . . .

At lunchtime I went to the little park on 53rd
Street and sat in a chair facing the waterfall that
drowns the city noises, staring at the water falling
endlessly down the smooth rock wall: all my tears. I
cried, just a little, but inside I felt the endless waterfall, water falling: not out, but pumped back up by
some artifice, some mechanical device, to fall again
down the smooth wall. Waterfall, water wall. Water
walling; water welling. Welling and falling.

The devil. Perhaps it is he with whom I make my
pact, and who gives me freedom to be as enraged, as
irrational, as destructive as I like. Sold my soul—my
freedom—for the right to be alone and angry and
hate-filled. Freedom to be or feel; a one-sided freedom: freedom from the old, but in a new bondage to
this new devil.

Razor blades, lines on wrists, cutting over the bathroom
sink or tub: I began collecting not just pieces of glass but
bottles; and these I'd throw against the tiles, and then smash
and smash myself on the pieces against the hard bathroom
surfaces. Already in early July I was preparing for the doctor's vacation in August. ("He writes down for me the dates
of his disappearance.") I was killing him, killing myself,
again and again. Instead of writing blood and destruction I
became it.

Kill, kill. Destroy. That is my life feeling: destruction. I don't feel any other. Maybe once I knew another, but it is so far away, so far gone that it has no
meaning. There is no past to recapture. Only the intolerable present.

[Some hours later] What did I do? tried to kill you, and my right hand is nearly unusable. The pain. Crying in the middle of the wreckage, the carnage, and going on; and still the soft white untouched, un-mutilated parts of my body make me sick, as sick as the blood and the pain and the horrible mess on the floor. This time I do not, cannot, clean it. How many bottles? why count? a terrible gush: there is a hole in the wrist, gashes in the hand, seeming to be tinged with green glass . . . It's me breaking, smashing, cutting you, and you come back at me murderously . . . All my clothes are stained with blood. A gash on the knee . . . Let me sleep. In the stench and filth of blood: of terror.

I sit stuck to this chair wondering what I am doing, what I think I am doing, what I have been doing for the past five hours. Tell me that. You, doctor. Answer me, she screams. Have you seen this progression from the very beginning, known that at the crucial moment of balance on the tightrope you would leave me. Destroyer and savior. I know, I call you my tormentor, when it is not you at all, when it is myself. It is not you who walks down Lafayette Street smashing your already bloody hand through whiskey bottles in the gutter; picking the windows you will assault on the next dark night, the next gray dawn. Those ragged men lying in doorways—they wouldn't stop me. Dripping with blood I walked, and no one said a word.

Images: tightrope, abyss; doctor as devil, doctor as tormentor; me a marionette on a string controlled by him. Roaches. Blood and glass.

Every day I get up and wonder, what would I do if I were not to see the doctor tonight. Every day like to-day when I wake with a sort of shudder and trembling; when I fall asleep in a fright, thinking I do not want to sleep, do not want to wake up, do not want to think of the hours in the morning before work, the way to work, work itself. As if I am holding a body in my hand, have it in my control, and must do something with it. Wash it, dress it, give it food, walk or ride it that distance to its office.

I made myself an expert in bottles, the different kinds, thicknesses, shapes, colors; and different ways of breaking them; and the different vulnerabilities of parts of the body: where to get the most blood, most pain. Also in where to break them: tired of the mess in my apartment, I went out: to alleys, vacant lots, run-down parts of the city, at deserted times of day, dark or early morning. I would arrive smashed and bloody at the doctor's.

The doctor said, "You want to break everything you see because that's how you feel: broken, torn, shattered." He had not understood: "I don't just break a bottle, I smash it again and again into splinters with my arms, wrists, head." "You feel like breaking everything in this room," he said.

I began to watch for the doctor's car, to see what street he took downtown from his house to his office, where he parked. It was another version of trying to imagine him when he was not in his office: in the hospital; in his apartment, his weekend house, with his family. His secretary knew my voice. One night I sat across the street from his building and waited for him to go home: I watched him arrive, park, go into the building. After he went in I broke a bottle in front of his car. It was just before his vacation.

While he was gone, I was to see Dr. S. at Brookdale once a week. In the meantime I wrote the doctor long letters; or maybe it was all one letter. In the middle of his vacation he came back to see me, for two hours on a Friday morning. On my lunch hour that day I went to an abandoned house I knew—in midtown, Tudor City—and smashed my hand; it turned out that I had cut a tendon. For the first time I went to a hospital emergency room; I had to have stitches. But it didn't stop me. "I have a body, but it's fragments."

It was September; the doctor's vacation was over. We have four hours a week, he said. "We'll see what we can do, and if it doesn't work there's always the hospital." He also agreed to end the family sessions. To me this was a great relief. I had dreaded and hated them; they were a wall between me and myself, me and the doctor: an interruption.

He said: "It is I who must take care of you, not you taking care of yourself, holding yourself. Break the glass here, cut yourself here; let me take care of you. Don't do it before you come or when you leave; try just to do it here." When I arrived cut up at his office, he washed the wounds and bandaged them; if he thought they needed stitches he took me to an emergency room or, once, to a doctor around the corner from his office. "Doesn't your doctor think you should be in the hospital?" this doctor said.

> The doctor has become such a demon, bad-demon and good-demon, that I cannot write much of him. And all I write, or would write, is of him. I lose him, lose touch, much more quickly than I did . . . Be, be; be without thinking. Let the couch replace your mind. But it is all a series of entrances and exits: almost before the entrance is the exit. I will never stop smashing glass, because I will never reach whatever it is I am wanting to reach, not without dying. Dying:

it's a slow word. Not without killing myself. What are
you feeling, I ask myself; and the answer is Nothing. I
knew without asking. Well, that's not quite right; it is
the instant answer. But the deeper answer is that I
feel strained, nervous—it is going to come soon, the
insanity, the madness. Oh stop writing Grace. It does
no good. It does bad. Bad for you. Straining to reach
whatever I is—yourself; pure being. Feeling. Without
thinking. I walk into my house and I sit down at the
typewriter. And nothing comes out. NOTHING. I
scream because even the writing is saying nothing.
Expressing what is not expressible; I don't even know
what it is that is wanting to be expressed—wanting to
be reached. You want to cut through to the heart? But
she sits silently tearing at her hair.

It is as if I don't think about her, Susan, for a long
time, and then suddenly I am filled with her; but I
think that is only a seeming; I think that really I am
thinking about her all the time. Her and the doctor.
The rest, they have all receded, they are all on the
surface that falls off when I enter this room. The skin
that is shed . . . Take a pill; two pills. The whole
bottle of pills. Then you really wouldn't wake up. But
I want to be there when they light the memorial can-
dle, on the day, and all its anniversaries. I don't want
to die; I just want to be insane, watch them carrying
me away. Does this person who calls himself a doctor
really think he can do anything about me?

For a mind without a body she talks a lot about
it; thinks a lot about it. You've got it: exactly the
point. If there were not such a separation you would
not hear so much about the pieces of skin, the puddles of blood, the band-aids and the shapes of scars.

Susan in my thoughts and images stands for the doctor: and everything he is.

I am, literally, not intact. My body is full of holes.

The Glory of Glass; The Glory That Was Glass: I made up titles for myself.

At the doctor's I lie on the couch; cry; beat my fists against the wall. Near the fireplace he keeps a brown paper bag of bottles that I brought, and in the desk drawer a supply of band-aids and butterfly sutures (given to him by me). By mid-September I was able to take out my own stitches.

Grace at the doctor's: silly and then disgusted: sad and suddenly raging and violent, destroying the felt, the soft, touchable—by the doctor—sadness of the moment before. It is as if the moment before was a dream: a daze: something that never happened. And yet, he says, it is this rage that is the nightmare that drives you crazy.

Exit from the doctor's office, exit from the doctor. You know what I am going to do; it's only a question of whether I do it here or in the street. I get up to leave; he holds me: was I shaking? Do you feel me holding you? Yes, and I cannot let myself; if I do, it is all over. I will be crazy. I CAN'T LET GO. Shall I call you at nine? I don't know . . . yes. Is it worse if I call? I don't know. Well, for what it's worth, I will call you . . . For what it's worth: those are the words that are pasted in my mind. He lets me go; I can go only because I did not let go. What form will it take, the destruction that is to come? I am not going to kill myself; but there is going to be blood. You know that.

Sometimes when I leave I run; sometimes I seem to be in a daze. Eventually I get to one of my dark alleys or doorways and smash myself. Also after eating; seeing people; sometimes just talking on the phone. Anatomical experiments: after wrists and arms the head, hips, legs. As things got bloodier and intenser in the doctor's office, sometimes even I thought of the hospital, as the only possible containment: physical.

The doctor says, You have to keep cutting yourself. Go on cutting yourself; you have to remain in touch with your body, with yourself, in whatever way you can.

Sometimes, magically, with his hands, he does make the pain go away. Makes magic with his hands. Mobile, that is another word for those hands. He talks with his hands; and then there is his voice . . . Last night I tried very hard and I felt again the hand in my hair, laying me to rest. Peace, he said; you want peace, not death; but if death is the only way—I will understand.

It is like the saddest of sad songs; ballads; pieces, and touching. Being in pieces, being in touch. In touch with the pieces of the body.

I want to appear in naked slices before him. How can this be, this terrible effect.

Anatomy of a Wrist.

Try not to cut yourself, he says again and again; it becomes almost a plea. Is he sick of bandaging my wounds? There is no need; I can take care of it all myself now . . . I am trying, I say; I really am. Yes I am trying; but the bottles, the sight of glass, of blood on glass, of gashes, has become a real part of me: the sight, the feel, the smell, the knowledge, of both bottles and anatomy.

Images: drowning with you the person who is trying to save you; the hospital gown of calm; cutting off my hands, or feet.

My mother calls the doctor to see how I am doing.

In mid-October I'd gone to stay at the apartment of a friend while she was in Europe. There was a new neighborhood to explore; and an electric typewriter: I wrote 35 pages in a week.

The feeling of dependence on the doctor becomes intense, suffocating: that he is my life, I am trapped. The blurring of boundaries: who is it I want to destroy, who is it that does the destroying? Fear of killing him—isn't that really why you wanted to cut off your hands?

Violence against him: My brown bag is still in his office; maybe in the morning he will get there first, or I will wait until he is inside, before I go in, armed, to tear myself and him to shreds; to pieces.

I don't know why I go on seeing you, he said. The experience must mean something to me, though I couldn't say what. We're in it together.

Living with Life.

I call the scenes that pass through my head visions, but they are not, not any more than dreams. I call the different selves voices, I call the doctor devil, but none of this prevents me from total control: from being able to go to work every morning looking more or less normal, whether I come from a nightmare or a cloud or the devil's chamber. All that wasted strength. I won't eat right and I won't sleep right and now I am on a campaign to physically use up or wear out my body by any means I can devise.

I made a vow to cut myself every day for a week: back to razor blades.

"When pushed to the wall, she has a perfect grasp of reality," the doctor says to my mother.

Essay on True Life.

The mother who *is* there.

You have to stop cutting yourself or you are going to cut yourself off from me, he said. It was early November. He must have been getting close to the edge of his endurance. ("Go wash your hands; *I'll* take care of this." There was glass all over his office, and the next patient was about to arrive.) The hospital is mentioned: but I become "good" when he sounds serious: a threat.

But I do want to escape; to get out.

You want to find peace; rest; within yourself, even if it means dying.

Yes, to find peace, rest, I carve myself, deeper and deeper reaching inside.

You don't have to die; try simply to be; you are reexperiencing something important; only try to do it without blood. (You see, I am not a very good doctor, he says. He wants to say the cut should be sutured, but he covers the two deep almost jagged cuts with the plastic strips.) I know I repeat myself, he says, but I must; you must take that risk of believing me, believing in me, believing I do not want to lose touch with you. It has to be this way for a while, this exclusiveness of the world, this making of a world that exists only between you and me. Forever, I say. Of course: from where you are you must see it that way. Even from these cuts there is not much blood; how does one bleed to death? There: he touches the pulse; that is the main artery: you would have a hard time stopping the bleeding. But I have given him the razor blades: symbolically.

I do not want to go to the hospital; but don't want not to. That is, I wished I could be taken out of the world, out of my life: and left to be.

A battlefield, he said of my wrist.

More and more, I began to live in that "exclusive" world of myself and the doctor.

> You know, I said, you are much more with me than it may appear. It seems I don't trust you, seems I hold back from you, refuse to believe you, reach out to you; but you are always in me, always with me . . . I am talking to you at every moment of the day. Dialing your number and saying nothing, but really I am talking all the time to you . . . I never forget you. I think of you waiting at the end of the day or of the night, and in that is a sort of survival. You have to take the risk sometime, with someone: being held without even knowing that you are being held. Oh I wish it could be true! Wish by speaking the words I made them true: but speaking them almost seems to do the opposite, to set the feeling farther out of reach . . . Sometimes I feel you are saying I offer myself, everything I have, everything I am, and you will not take it, will not respond. And of course what follows is that you leave me, drop me, abandon me. "Don't cut yourself." And I cut myself.

The doctor rescues me from Metropolitan Hospital. I didn't do a very good job, the surgeon said. Do you get mad when you see people like me? I asked. No, he said. They all do it to themselves one way or another.

> Doctor: Your whole body must be in terrible pain, so out of touch with itself. (How does he know to say that?) It takes a lot of courage to hack away at yourself to find your real, your true self.

All these little cuts, they are nothing: polite quiet little scratches meaning nothing compared to what you really feel: cutting off your hands, cutting yourself to pieces.

What is blood, what does it mean? I think it is that, the power over the body, over my life, fusion of self and solitude, detached, isolated from everything, everyone: me, myself, and I. FREE.

About cutting: I always know . . . except in the moment of its happening: though even then I'm knowing, I know . . . no . . . I know and don't know at the same time. It starts and then I can't stop; I am utterly caught, trapped, in the bottle or in the razor blade, wildly smashing and cutting myself to pieces. All for you. And why, when you know, and I know you know . . . for you who are me who does not know.

Oh help me . . . I will trust you: I obey when you say come away from the glass, come and lie on the couch. You do control me, but only when you are present. You say, Don't cut yourself; but away from you your words do not stop me. They have no meaning, no sense. Nothing does, only what you call hacking away to find the self: literally. And it will not, does not, cannot stop.

Toward the end of November I came to a session carrying a long fluorescent light bulb with its end broken off:

When I came in, carrying it, crumbling off bits from the jagged end, crumbling them in my hand, you said, You know I have no more of those strips. You think I care? Incredulous. Or is that a veiled threat of the hospital. The way you left me yesterday, not dropped but torn from you. For many hours I resisted the impulse to blood, but I came out of the subway and there it was, this long poison-filled light bulb, and hardly knowing or thinking I was carrying it down Park Avenue. Notice how people often carry long rolled-up things under their arms: why shouldn't I. So. You are angry and in pain and restless, this is what you are telling me, yet somehow in control, you want to smash it or throw the handfuls of hand-crushed powdery glass at me but do not. Maybe you can talk about it. You sound like a schoolteacher, I say bitterly. That's terrible, you cry. For once really surprised. A schoolteacher . . . but after all I am a child. One crash against shoulder or knee or just in my hands, and then the table, where I stab and stab myself: warmth of my blood, clotting on the glass tabletop. I make a drawing, a finger painting on the glass . . . Now you are beside me on the floor, taking the glass from me, and I am left, as I always am, with the pitiful small cut that is nothing. I begin to cry. You too know the meaninglessness of that mere scratch. I follow you to the couch, where you sit close beside me, around me, covering me with your body. I hardly feel it. I wanted to grab the glass from you, screaming, go on stabbing, screaming at you, don't stop me. I obey, meekly. After a while you say Lie there; I am going to clean it up. I lie with my eyes hidden. Sound of the glass being thrown into the wastebasket. I feel it, that sound, in my stomach. You are throwing me away.

I hate you, but I know I don't hate you; I hate having to relive whatever this experience is—from the prehistory, preconsciousness of self—and to wonder how long it is going to go on.

I must have the razor blades, for tonight or for tomorrow morning or for tomorrow night when I go to see you. You haven't seen that, me with a razor blade. Plain and pure and direct and so simple. Reliving, acting out the experience. Why does it have to be acted out? And yet talking is obviously of no use. Or is like the scratches, an indication, a mere glimpse or sight or signal of what I feel, scratching of surfaces.

Reason enough to fall into a stuporlike sleep: to avoid having to kill myself. I don't want to be dead. But he is going to watch, the doctor, YOU, you are going to know better than words, better than light bulbs, better than pus-ridden wounds already inflicted.

By the next night I had gotten my razor blades; and perhaps, walking around the office with them, I really would have cut myself, and even the doctor. In any case the threat was so vivid that he had to stop me, and said I must go to the hospital. I pleaded with him, but he insisted. I suppose by now he had had enough; and maybe I had, too.

o

## A Basic Unity

### (Dr. Nakhla)

After Grace's discharge from her first hospitalization, in March, there was a rapid and dramatic change in the treatment ambience. Her terrifying feelings of nonexistence, which had been held tightly in check by her withdrawal and almost catatonic stillness and silence over the previous eighteen months, were at last in the open. She was visibly frightened; she found it difficult to remain seated in her chair and paced restlessly around the office. The atmosphere and the feelings between us were tense, charged; and the tension was heightened by the increased frequency of the sessions. I made comments about her feelings of fragmentation and destructiveness, but I also was anxious; I felt impelled to comfort her physically, to contain and restrain her.

In a way, the tension and anxiety were a welcome change from the many months of silence. Something seemed to be happening, and I felt that I was taking part in it. The incident of the shredded newspaper and the smashing of the clay pot was a long-awaited breakthrough. I understood it as, in Winnicott's terms, the handing over to the analyst of the false, caretaker self and the possibility of reaching the true self.

Of course, Grace's breakup with Susan had also precipitated this change in her condition and her relationship to me. In fact, she was able to tell me, years later, how her unity with Susan had contributed to her silence in the sessions: talking would bring the fear that it was not her voice and thoughts but Susan's, along with the fear that this would break up her relationship with Susan. I was reminded of Little's statement that "an existing folie-à-deux has to be destroyed for the analysis to be carried out" (1958, p. 3). She also says that the ensuing transference is often of a psychotic nature, accompanied by a delusional identity with the analyst.

Over the weeks, and especially before my vacation in August, Grace had been behaving in a more distraught manner in my office. Yet very little was communicated verbally, and even her obviously agitated behavior, such as pacing and crying, was not directed at me but seemed to be expressed in a void. I tried to remain as calm as possible, and also connected, by acknowledging what I thought she was experiencing. On a number of occasions when she was crying or appeared unusually tense, I went and sat quietly next to her or put my hand on her head or shoulder. I prescribed for her an antianxiety medication (Librium).

Grace communicated very little about her life, what she was going through, or her feelings about me. Consequently, I did not know the extent of her destructive behavior—the smashing of bottles in the streets or at home and the scratching of her wrists with razor blades and pieces of glass. Nor was I aware of how important I had become for her and how she tried to imagine me and hold me in her mind at every moment between sessions.

Before leaving for a four-week vacation, I told Grace that I would be back in the city for a day in the middle of it and arranged to see her at that time. I did not understand then that what I thought would be helpful would turn out to be profoundly traumatic for her. She did not yet have a stable internalized sense of me and thus could only feel totally overwhelmed by my appearing and disappearing. Right after the session she inflicted her first serious wrist cut and severed a tendon. She took care of it herself by going to a hospital emergency room.

Toward the end of the vacation I received a letter from her. She wrote:

> Dr. S. once said I was afraid of my own blood,
> the sight of it. Between the two of you, you really had
> me, caught between hate and fear. But tonight you
> can both be proud. I just let it drip or flow. I wish
> you could see the floor. My abhorrence of the melo-
> dramatic will not let me soak this page in it, though I
> am tempted. . . . Arms encrusted with dried blood
> and splinters of glass. It was not very good glass after
> all. I will have to go back to my deserted little house,

that and the razor blades. A quick deep swipe and
you get a lake of blood. But now I've cleaned it up,
the blood part, because it will make me sick. First,
though, like a child, I make you a finger painting. . . .
I am going to try to escape. I don't know where, but I
think it's going to be solitary. In the middle ages they
would have said I was possessed. Well I feel it coming on again.

Further in the letter (it had been written over several days
and was more a diary than a letter):

You know I am writing all these words to keep
myself from doing something. The nameless something. Maybe, I should/could just go back to razor
blades; it is less messy than bottles. But they don't
take care of the violence, unless one becomes unconscious—and that's the same as being asleep—you just
wake up with the violence unappeased, unmitigated
even, unless the blood or the scars make you sick.
Am I writing to you? You I can feel when I am being
held, when your hand is on my head, or in mine . . . I
don't know. It seems I am writing in or into a vacuum—an emptiness. Can emptiness be made of
pieces—torn-up pieces, shattered fragments. It always
seemed to me a wholeness—like a clear sky, a round
colorless clear sky.

Enclosed with the letter was her finger painting: a full page
completely covered on both sides with thick bloody en-
crustations, including splinters of glass.

I now realized how isolated Grace had been in her
turmoil and how destructively she had been acting out her
state of fragmentation. I had been interpreting her anxieties
of breakdown while attempting to support and rely on her
ability to take care of herself. The sessions with her parents

were in the way, keeping the focus on the fact that she continued to function smoothly in her day-to-day life. What she needed to feel was that I was totally there for her. When we resumed our sessions, I was not sure what to expect, but before I knew it I found myself with her in what she describes as being on a tightrope or hanging over an abyss. This life-and-death struggle continued for the next three months.

I reread Little's theoretical and clinical papers "On Basic Unity" (1960) and "On Delusional Transference (Transference Psychosis)" (1958) and Winnicott's writings, particularly his paper "Metapsychological and Clinical Aspects of Regression within the Psycho-Analytic Set-Up" (1954b). Both authors emphasize that bodily happenings become central to the analysis and that the analyst must tolerate acting out and actively play a part in it. The experiences can—and must—be interpreted at a verbal level, but only later, when the patient has gained the capacity for symbolic and deductive thinking. There is regression to absolute dependence, or to what Little terms a state of "basic unity."[1] She defines this as a psychic undifferentiatedness between patient and analyst; that is, the patient's belief in the analyst's total identity with him or her. In this condition, the patient is exposed temporarily to states of

1. Little's "basic unity" is a more apt term than the more widely used "symbiosis" (Mahler 1963, 1968) and "therapeutic symbiosis" (Searles 1965, 1979a). I describe Little's views of the differences in the clinical appendix to this volume. Symbiosis, a metaphor derived from biology, is misleading and implies a mutual bond and need on the part of both partners. Winnicott (1971a, p. 130) and R. Gaddini (1987, p. 329) have found the term unacceptable; Modell (1968, pp. 33–35) prefers to describe such a state of relatedness as a "transitional object relationship." Closely related to the concept of basic unity is Milner's notion of an "undifferentiated union" and Eigen's term "dual union," which are discussed by Eigen (1983) and Milner (1987, pp. 289–92).

depersonalization, which are experienced as chaos and annihilation. There is the awareness of one thing only—distress or pain of such overwhelming intensity that everything is annihilated, including any sense of being a person,
even a person suffering. Little describes how the fear of
annihilation and the drive to establish identity with the
analyst lead the patient both to avoid these states of depersonalization and at the same time to seek them, at any cost
to himself or the analyst.

Grace describes those experiences exactly in the diary
letter she sent me on my vacation:

> For months I have been teaching myself to turn to
> you, to think of you rather than Susan, and I have
> succeeded, to my own destruction. I think you have
> made a terrible mistake. You took me at a time of my
> life when I was most vulnerable, most weak, and you
> made me close to you, closer to you than anyone else
> in the world: *you made my existence not just depen-
> dent on you, but you made it you.* [My emphasis]

She continues:

> Without you I could have quietly cut myself off
> from life. Maybe I would be dead, but I might be dead
> soon enough anyway. But you changed that. Fuck.
> Now the bond is incredibly painful. It is *your* hand.
> You did it. You smashed that piece of glass.

At another point she writes:

> Oh, I know one sentence does not follow the
> next, but I am allowed this confusion with you. Con-
> fusion reminding me of other of my rages and
> screams at you . . . though really they are all con-
> tained in being dependent, and in wanting you to tell

me what I am doing—and how I can kill myself, without first killing you.

Grace's sense of unity with me and her sense of separateness from me were experienced in concrete, bodily terms. She wrote in her diary, referring to the ends of a cut tendon in her wrist:

> You cutting yourself off from me—my interpretation or manifestation or making physical (real) of that. And the other end of it, hidden far away, somewhere in the depths of my arm—that's you: you, whom I do not see, do not feel. The me part is pure pain. How's that for analysis—after-the-fact analysis, but poems are always analyzed after they are written, people (acts) are analyzed after they have been done (grown up). Perhaps that is something I have never understood. But why the need for analysis at all—that's something built-in, something not to be removed—only now my analysis takes various violent and destructive forms. But of course those forms are acts, reaction—not analysis—and I'm sick of the analysis of them. I just want you to tell me something, tell me anything.

It is almost impossible, even at this time, or perhaps because of the passage of time, to describe or to reflect dispassionately on my feelings and actions during that period. Grace's diary documents many of them, and her account in the preceding chapter conveys something of what we went through. Her reporting of my statements and reactions (which I did not record) brings back painful memories of those frightening times and the reliving of the disturbing range and intensity of feelings. My responses were shifting and contradictory—at times sounding like pleas or threats—and thus reflected the overwhelming strain and the bewildering effort to convey to Grace the *sense* of my being totally there for her while at the same time stepping back, being separate and whole in myself, and leaving her with her life and body in her own hands.

The end of each session and the period between sessions were as stressful for me as they were for Grace. I recognized and accepted, without fully comprehending, that in Grace's state of absolute identity with me she was incapable of reaching for me when she was away from my office. This left me preoccupied and anxious about whether she was in danger. I tried to deal with this according to both what I thought she needed and my own emotional needs by scheduling telephone calls. Little quotes remarks by one of her patients: "I find I haven't told you something, and that is because I thought you already knew it," and "It's so much easier to talk to you when you aren't really there than when you are" (1960, p. 382).

The overriding force that sustained my commitment to Grace's treatment was the conviction that she was coming to life. Her physical pain, destructive rage, and self-mutilations and the sight of her blood all made her feel not only alive but real, and connected to her body. I also knew that I was vital to the process. In spite of the enormous strain and danger, I believed that the alternative of interrupting what was happening would be worse. Perhaps I was struggling with these emotions when I said to Grace: "I don't know why I go on seeing you. The experience must mean something to me, though I couldn't say what. We're in it together."

Grace's wrist cutting seemed to bring us together in a state of psychic oneness, but at the same time, inevitably, it defined our separateness. These feelings were perpetuated by the healing wounds. I came to recognize, with a sense of relief, that while a wound was healing there was less risk of further cutting. In fact, at these times Grace appeared calmer and more connected to me; she had a certain awareness of her body and seemed to care for it. On occasion she would ask me to look at a wound and the sutures, to assure her that it was healing properly.

I turned repeatedly to the writings of Winnicott and Little for guidance and support and in the hope of finding an "answer." In her paper "On Delusional Transference" (1958), Little emphasizes that the state of basic unity is the unconscious basis of the transference phenomena and that the analyst must accept it fully, being psychically indistinguishable from the patient yet preserving a personal identity. She continues:

> He must find what he feels right for himself (i.e. what he wants to do or say), and assume that it is equally right for the patient. It is a point at which he must be able to commit himself, even sometimes risking making a mistake, but remembering that the biggest mistake of all at this point may be *not* doing just this. (p. 5)

In the final paragraph of the paper she writes:

> I have talked about "what" and "why," rather than about "how." The "how" is not easily described in ways that convey meaning. Once one begins to describe ways of doing things that are unfamiliar to one's hearers anxiety is inevitably aroused, with consequent misunderstanding and distortions. We have to rely largely on empathy, which *is* relying on this basic state, but enlarged by experience. Each of us has to find his own "how," by trial and error, letting happen what happens in himself, and finding out for himself the realities of analysis.

Although I did not find an answer, it was helpful to recall that both Little and Winnicott describe the tremendous management difficulties and dangers to the patient as well as to the analyst involved in working with the severely regressed patient. I thought back to comments such as Little's:

> The analyst's own instinctual impulses have to be used as fully and directly as possible. Very primitive emotions are suddenly aroused in him, often leaving him no time for conscious thought before he has to speak or act. Provided his own analysis has gone far enough for sublimations to be established; provided he is mature, knows his limitations, and is not depending on or exploiting his patient, the dangers which are admittedly there are fair risks, especially considering the seriousness of the illness. (1958, p. 3)

Finally, in a session in November 1975, I reached my limit and told Grace that she must go to the hospital. A few days earlier she had cut her wrist, and that evening in my office she was clutching a razor blade and pacing the floor in a menacing way. She appeared quite mad to me, and I felt threatened by her. When I moved to my desk to make arrangements for hospitalization, her behavior changed abruptly. She looked frightened, and sat at my feet promising that she would be good and not cut herself. I told her that I did not want her to make such promises but that I needed her to be hospitalized because I had to have some relief. The hospital had no beds, but the admitting physician offered to keep Grace overnight in the seclusion room.

# 5
# Second Hospitalization

(November–

December 1975)

o

## A Containment

**(Grace Jackson)**

I remember going to the hospital. The doctor
had called my parents, and we waited in his office until
they came. I suppose he called the hospital, too. While we
waited he had to send a patient away; I heard her say: "As
long as *you're* all right, doctor . . ."

For three days I was in the seclusion room, with constant observation. A nurse sat outside the closed door. What
I remember is blankness: lying on the bed (or mattress) half
sleeping, staring at nothing. Not violent; maybe even peaceful—later it seemed a symbol of a blank peaceful state
(although peaceful implies something almost positive; un-

disturbed, maybe, or still; physically and mentally silent, inactive). The doctor came to see me; we smoked a cigarette. I didn't eat; I only drank juice. I had a cut on my wrist that was infected and had to be taken care of. They always said I was "suicidal," which was a simple, easy way of explaining my being there. I suppose I looked it: "pale, emaciated-looking, not well groomed" (according to the hospital record), with wrist cuts and scars. I never thought myself that I was suicidal (but then I didn't see my physical self clearly: after all, it had no reality for me, no connection to me); yet what was going on between me and the doctor was too complicated to explain. And maybe, as I said, we both needed a rest.

Nurses, doctors, other therapists were always trying to talk to you, get you to talk about yourself, about your problems, but this time the doctor told them to leave me alone; and I also was not compliant, as I had been my first time in the hospital.

> Seclusion-room nurses' notes: "Offered no complaint;
> refused shower; refused breakfast; drank plenty of
> fluids; pleasant on approach; slept intermittently
> throughout shift; very reluctant to verbalize . . . n.b.
> two pieces of broken bottle found in pt.'s handbag."

I remember going in a wheelchair from the 13th floor (where the seclusion room was) to the 5th floor, my belongings (clothes I came in, handbag) on my lap, still in a kind of daze. I was put in the room opposite the nursing station, on constant observation; here the door was open, and a nurse was always sitting in the doorway. The room had two beds, in opposite corners, with a big window in between and a narrow windowsill. The bathroom was on the hall side; if you were on C.O. they took the lock off the door. I don't remember very much about the first days; I mostly stayed in my room, on my bed or looking out the window; reading or staring at nothing, listening to the voices from the nurses' station: not the words but the sounds. There was a long view over Brooklyn from those windows, as far as the Verrazano Bridge. One night—the second night—I was looking out and someone told me to get away from the windowsill. I was furious, raging. They thought I was going to jump. They held me down and gave me a shot. I wasn't going to jump, I only wanted to look out and be left alone; being interfered with—and not under-stood—just made me more violent. There was a woman who insisted that I was her daughter, Sharon. I got angry and screamed at her, again and again. Other patients, nurses tried to reason with her; once they even arranged for us to talk to each other (but this must have been much later). I felt persecuted by her, this sad old lady who followed me crying Sharon, Sharon, and at mealtimes would bring a chair for me. I didn't have any sense of myself anyway, and this seemed to confirm it, this being taken for someone else. The only real connection I felt was with the doctor: as it had been before the hospital. Lost in myself, I waited for him to come; he would sit with me, sometimes put his hand on my head, and I would feel more connected to myself, that I did exist, although not separate from him. Being connected to the doctor is being connected to myself.

After the initial, almost dazed state, the adult part of you begins to return and you hate the hospital, you want only to get out of it. And so eventually I began to come out of my room, to talk to some of the nurses and other patients. At the same time you perceive how weak you are, and are afraid to leave. For the first two weeks, I didn't even write. Then maybe I started to make pots. The dayroom was a long yellowish room with windows along one wall, facing southwest. At the far end was a big wooden table, the OT (occupational therapy) table; there was a potter's wheel and other stuff around. At the near end were the tables for meals and a TV. After a while I began staying up late, playing Scrabble, watching TV. I think it began because the light bothered my roommate when I was reading and she was trying to sleep. Gloria: she had just had a baby and had tried to throw herself out the hospital window. A large young slow-moving slow-witted girl with strawlike hair. (But maybe the slowness was because of the drugs.) One night in the bathroom she broke a perfume bottle and tried to cut her wrists. (Maybe that's when they took the lock off the door.) I was extremely upset. It seems to me, looking back, that, good and bad, these were all interactions—as they would say. That the ward really does have a life of its own, there is no solitude, no shelter. The old ladies, depressed, had mostly swallowed bottles of pills. Maybe they were already embarrassed.

There was an electric typewriter on the OT table and I started typing, at night, into the night, afraid to sleep or that I wouldn't be able to sleep. It was just like old times in my apartment, writing myself into chaos, so that I would end up with broken glass or a razor blade. In the hospital you couldn't have the same resolution; in a way not being able to write, or think, had been a relief. From that diary:

> I wish I could simply go to sleep—at least there was
> that relief when I first came, the relief of almost never
> leaving the bed, weakness of body and mind . . . It's
> dawns you like, isn't it, the dr said. One day last
> week I was talking about those changes from dark to
> light to dark that break the day or night, how I haven't
> been able to see them, those changes that affirm
> one's existence, those markings of time. Here I pur-
> posely do not watch the sunset: there is something
> painful about the passing of a day in which you seem

not to have participated: which you have, rather,
watched through a window, or not watched.

Everyone was fascinated by my writing, wanted to know if
I was writing a book, a book about the ward; making a sort
of joke of it, I said I was.

My sister Eleanor and Jim, her boyfriend, came on the
bus from Oregon to see me.

Once you emerge from your room, once you open your
eyes, you could say, the tediousness of hospital life is tremendous. Maybe it's boredom that makes you start partic-
ipating: doing OT, talking (or listening) to other patients,
to the nurses (it was just before Christmas, they were full
of shopping, presents, plans), playing games (Scrabble,
bingo: one day I won a pair of bright-green plastic earrings),
watching TV, even, finally, going on a trip. (Doctors appear
and disappear; nurses are part of daily life, they talk about
families, errands, events in their lives, as people would in
any office.) It's like nursery school, or camp; and these
activities can seem almost insulting to an adult self (the
very word "activities"). But in an important way you don't
have an adult self; I didn't. Let's say I didn't have a body;
in a kind of condensed way you grow up all over again.
The hospital can't really let you do this at your own pace;
nor do you want it to. A point comes when all you want is
to go home. I said I was homesick and wanted to go home,
yet felt that I had no home. That was the paradox: "All I
know is I am sick of this life that can hardly be called life—
but what am I wanting? I look out on the wet streets, the
springlike December air, and wonder what they can hold
for me. It's not a question, he (the doctor) said once, of
whether the world is there: look out, you see it; the question
is whether you are, or can be, in it." When I did leave, it
wasn't to go home, or even to a sense of going home, but
to a controlled, caretaking situation: to live with my sister

Martha. I went out on a day pass with her; I remember both the feeling of being outside for the first time in weeks (except for walking across a parking lot to and from an interview with Dr. Frank, a consultant psychoanalyst)—the excitement of air and movement, and also the humiliation of having to be watched, accompanied the whole time. I hated it, yet I knew—I felt—the need for it. Then I went out with my parents, driving. We got out of the car in Flushing to have lunch. The sidewalk glittered: glass, immediately I could touch it, feel it, feel blood, see the wound. From my diary:

> A slow process this business of recovery. I do not
> walk outside and find that the sight of glass shining
> in the cracks of the sidewalk is a distant and terrible
> nightmare from which I have finally waked. No—it is
> as close and tormenting as ever, and it is only some
> great force of will that is going to keep me from it . . .
> I notice . . . how I listen for the aching of my scars,
> desperate sort of groping for the reality of physical
> pain.

> The Chronicle of Snapper 5:
> Do we have names or are we nameless? I assure
> you you are there and under your own names, and
> yes, of course, I am writing about Snapper 5: now
> speak a little louder—I didn't catch that last remark.
> Chapter 26: they are very short. Twenty-six came out
> of my mouth: looking for significance is easy, isn't it:
> my age. Twelve-thirty. It's the midnight shift, George
> is here, he says nothing about my typing. But the TV
> is on, and voices are louder than all the mechanical
> sounds. Henry, my "friend," is here, too. (He would
> let me type, whereas George could be harsh, strict. He
> wore an earring, before it was common.) The lights go

on: there is tuna fish from the Thursday night party.
Hello, secretary, calls George with a wave. He carries
a plate of food left from dinner. They stopped sending
staff trays in order to buy covers for the ovenproof-
plastic dishes.

"Chronicle" came to me in the night, one night
when I had been forced to turn out the light and lay
restless. Other words and even sentences form, all
forgotten now. I don't remember dreams so clearly anymore, only vague bits and pieces.

Linda comes to see what I am doing and tells me
the story of her life. It's all part of the therapy, learning to talk to strangers about the most intimate aspects of your self, your life. P. [resident doctor] is
also her doctor: she likes him and feels close up to
the point where he becomes for her "a man," and
then she backs away. Twenty-eight and three children: "If I did it again I would never have kids . . . I
just want to have fun . . . I know what I want but I
can't act on it. I want to go back to school, I want to
make a home for myself and my kids, I want to get
rid of my boyfriend." Boyfriend of seven years; a
house and three dogs and many cats. "But do I want
to get rid of him or is it my mother convincing me I
do? My mother who is quite old and has been
through a lot, at whom I can't get angry . . . I am an
excellent faker. I want to be sheltered and taken care
of, but I also want to live on my own. Many people
are strong and many are weak, and I'm one of the
weak. I want a good man who will take care of me
and love my kids. But you know men, when they
hear you have three kids, forget it. But I know what I
want; I just don't know if I can act on it, and that's
why the doctor's keeping me here. I was supposed to
go home: I don't know if I can take it." (A pretty red-

haired woman, soft-looking, with small features, thin lips. She became very close to another patient, Rick; when they left they were going to be together.) "Talking to everyone here I feel alive for the first time," she says. "Sounds crazy, doesn't it?" Not crazy at all: I wish I could say the same. They tell me it's true, that I am more alive, more real, and sometimes I do feel it myself; but when I transpose that self to the outside it seems to disintegrate at the merest brush or touch of another person, a feeling, an act.

One-thirty. Lin has gone to bed. It won't be a best-seller, she says with a laugh. It's without bitterness, that laugh. Even when she says she would do it differently if she could do it again there's no bitterness.

Sometimes the scars ache; sometimes there is a flash of pain as if the cut were being renewed: remade. A reminder of how I care for myself. Get it out, set it out, let the words run . . . out. They will never run out: there is always a new twist, a new typewriter, a new arrangement, a pencil and the back of an old envelope. How can you fail? Knowing the problem is half the battle, they say. Another favorite: God helps those who help themselves. They make me angry: they make all of "us" angry. The "psychological" questions anyone could ask. Two therapists say the same thing at the same moment in the group therapy session. They have studied the same textbook. Anyone can put the "why"s into a conversation, or say What's going on here? at the appropriate points. You want to scream, someone says. The foreign doctor who got the proverb wrong: What does it mean, You can't kill two birds with one stone? You can't, I would say.

Letter from Grace's sister Martha to Dr. Nakhla
(December 1975)

Dear Dr. Nakhla,

One day last week Eleanor and I went by ourselves to visit Grace. Usually she seems to me to be
like a person who lives in a lake and who by all her
screaming and typing and thrashing around has so
disturbed the muddy bottom that all she can see is
murk and terrifying shapes that scare her, and make
her thrash around and confuse things all the more.
But when Eleanor and I were there, for the very first
time she could, and would, distinguish shapes other
than the unrecognizable ones she stirs up herself. She
seemed to see, and more than that to admit, that
maybe there was not some great answer meant just for
her hiding in the mud at the bottom that would solve
everything and make her real if she could find it. It
seemed as though she could see that maybe everything just needed to slow down and settle from being
a filthy swirl to being something she could recognize
and take for her own. And I said to her that I really
hoped you made her stay in the hospital for a long,
distilling time, and she said, "Even though I hate it
here and am bored, and that lady thinks I'm her
daughter?" And we said yes, even with all those
things. So she said, very simply, "Well, you should
tell him."

I know that I don't understand Grace's sickness
for the most part, but it seemed for that one hour
there was a little bit of a chance that she could get
well, because she was really just one of three sisters
sitting at the table, and she wasn't trying not to be. So
I decided I would write to you, only really to tell you
that I'm glad Grace is in the hospital, that for this
while she is held in some kind of a thoughtful sus-

pension, where she doesn't have to type and tear herself up.

We went to see her on Tuesday night, too, and this time she was sick and thrashing up the mud again. She told us how she had begun typing again, and she said it arrogantly, as if to proclaim she was out to preserve her disease to make up for that painfully regular, sisterly visit when she hadn't needed to be different from us. This time when I told her I'd written you a letter she looked scared, as if something might come between you that would weaken her hold on you. She said could she see the letter, and I said yes, because she looked like a hunted animal. And if you do show it to her I suppose she will try and talk away whatever small conviction and confidence I meant it to have, and I know how good she is at doing that. But it is up to you whether you show it to her or not, and even if she manages to negate it, and talk her way back out into her world, I am glad I wrote it and glad I sent it.

# 6
# Without a Home

(January–September
1976)

○

## Finding My Mother

### (Grace Jackson)

I went to live with Martha and Will, her boyfriend: that was the agreement. I didn't want to; but I knew
that I had to: that I couldn't be by myself. The hospital had
calmed me, although when I first left I was afraid it might
be as false a calm as the other time. But now I wasn't by
myself.

I thought and wrote a lot about my childhood and my
family: trying to figure out where I came from. Or how I
got where I was. I tried to write my memories as stories. I
also tried to write about the hospital, to make sense of that.

I did stay up late at night to write, but not in the old way. I didn't have my own room: I slept on the couch or on the floor in the living room, and at night would type in the kitchen.

> I am so tired of the tightrope, I say. Better to jump or drop or fall into pieces than simply to wait for it to happen by itself. Something eludes me, some memory, some past Eden of the mind: was it real or was it never? It was always a precarious world. Even now I can sometimes gain or regain a certain peacefulness: but it is the peace of death, of walking in utter self-containment down a street, looking out through the glass walls—the windows—of myself, which the slightest move—a taxi honking, remark of a man in the street, someone walking too close in front of me or brushing me in passing—shatters. And so to deal with, to "cope," I must be shattered already, or enclosed in my block of ice. I go to the doctor and the ice begins to thaw a little; but it has to freeze as soon as I leave, and it seems that no progress is made. Only in the hospital could one be without windows: without boundaries . . . But what is that elusive burden of memory? What is she trying to grasp? Sometimes I sit with him, sit close beside him, even holding or being held . . . and I hear not a word he says; rather, I hear his voice passing around me, but none of the words penetrate, can be taken in, strain though I will . . . and I wonder, does he know? Often he knows me better than I. Am I sitting too far away? he asks. Yes; and he moves the chair closer. Yes: I felt it, and could articulate it not even to myself.

I would get restless, and frightened. I went for a walk and smashed my hand on a light bulb.

I always felt that I was clinging desperately to the edge of a cliff: the tightrope over the abyss and the edge of the cliff were my images. The cliff was the doctor: and I was always afraid I would not be able to hold on. The struggle was intense: life and death. I had survived—had been put into the container of the hospital—but now I was more conscious of what I was doing, or going through: now, I thought, if I kill myself it would be deliberate. I struggled to keep myself from cutting; and sometimes I didn't think the struggle was worth it.

And cutting? I haven't forgotten that. Or breaking an ashtray or the glass tabletop? Why do you think I sit on the couch, far away from all those dangerous things? I am protecting us, you and me.

I read: Trollope, Dickens—long nineteenth-century novels, which brought me into a completely different, safe world.

"What we are trying to do is very difficult," the doctor would say. And he also said: It will take a very long time.

The doctor is safe. I can say to him—I have learned to be able to say to him—I am pretending. I am not feel-ing, I am just talking. My words are meaningless. Right now he is somewhere between here and New Orleans, where he went to a conference, and anyway it would do me no good to speak to him. I have to be with him. And how dangerous even that would be, for I would not carry away any comfort, would want only to stay infantlike with him; held, infantlike, by him. I want to talk, and I cannot. Is there anyone to believe in? Not even myself, only in him.

I didn't like living at Martha and Will's; the apartment was too small for three—it was impossible to be alone. Even at night, when the others were asleep, I did not really feel alone there. I wanted my own room, my own things: I felt scattered, like my possessions: homeless. Yet I knew that, as the doctor said, it was a state of mind. I began spending some nights in my own house:

> My own house: I can come home with bloody hands and no one is there to see. The thought slipped out on my way home tonight. Is that my definition of safety? Invisibility? Inviolability? All the dreams about doors. The doctor who is both the intruder and the one whom I call on to save me.

Then, on an April weekend at my parents', I smashed my wrist, badly. I was taken screaming to the hospital, and all night I screamed for my mother, who stayed with me. It was as if I had finally smashed through to an infant self, completely dependent on my mother. And so now every weekend I went to my parents'; consciously I let myself— I made myself—become a child, and be taken care of by them.

> I am looking at my life, as if down a corridor, and it makes a strange sort of sense. The girl-becoming-woman, always unhappy, "depressed," almost to the point of its being a role that she could not escape and yet felt that no one believed; and in the other world, the world of home and parents, showing a serenity she knew she didn't feel. It seems inevitable that such a double falsehood should collapse, that such a foggy fantasy, such a loss, should end in blood—for what is more real, more tangible as self than blood, the substance that keeps one alive.

The doctor's car: I tell him about looking for his car, seeing where it's parked and trying to figure out from that

what route he took downtown. Or I would take the subway
to 96th Street and find where he had parked the night before
and figure out what route he had taken uptown. Then I
would walk downtown to his office; later, sometimes he
would see me walking and pick me up. If my session was
at night, I would take a roundabout subway route home.

> I do not want to go there [doctor's] tonight. All I
> can think of is the gold wallpapered door that has
> become a huge insurmountable obstacle.
> You [doctor] loom larger and larger, threatening
> to engulf me and so deny me. Blood.

I am trying to remember, to invest what has happened
to me with feeling, with emotion. I am trying in a sense to
relive my whole childhood, not to repossess but to possess
it for the first time. I spend hours creating memories or
scenes around photographs, around kitchen sinks or screen
doors.

> Last night the doctor said, "I regressed with Grace;
> I too felt the shock of walking out of the office into the
> air as if into another world." I was moved by his say-
> ing that. All his references to the past, to "what we
> have been through together": I didn't even know he
> was there with me; wouldn't know or realize or ac-
> cept it: no, I had to go on cutting and cutting, bleed-
> ing, without tears. I wonder, do I know it now?

I felt weak but violent. Or I felt empty, that I would
never have a self, experience myself, a life. I was waiting,
always waiting, I did not know for what. At the same time,
my job became more settled. I became a regular proofreader
and had a permanent office, which I shared with a woman
my own age. Sometimes I felt that my office was more a

home, a place or space of my own, than where I actually
lived.

In a corner [of the doctor's office] is the desk. There
are thin white curtains before the windows and long
heavy curtains that he draws in the early morning of
a hot day; and he pulls the shades down, too, to keep
the sun from making the room too hot. What a protective man he is.

In the doctor's office: I stood at the window and
wrapped myself in the curtain. What you really want,
he says, is not to kill me but simply to be bad, and
you are afraid that being bad means destruction. You
want to kill me but you also need me. Stuck. I am
sitting on the floor listening to him and suddenly I
can't stand it, the words, the sound of his voice. I
hate you; and I get up and walk away. I want so
much to break something, break it against his head. I
cry a little; whimper; nothing violent escapes me.

Finally he comes over to me, for I refuse to—cannot—cross the room to him. Let's try to deal with it a
different way, is the prelude. I let him put his arms
around me, make a semblance of holding me, but it is
only a semblance, for I am tightly holding on to myself and feel nothing. Impossible, hopeless, I cry, and
break away.

He kneels on the chair and I stand above him.
Why are positions so important? I mean to remember
that curtain; it protected me . . . I have flashes of hating him, succeeded by longings to see him: each state
understands the other not at all.

I don't want to go . . . don't leave . . . I won't go:
crying hysterically, clutching his arm. Yet I am hold-

ing an emptiness: I do not feel him, his presence,
comforting, holding, protecting. It's a desperate effort.

Finally, in the summer, I gave up my apartment; Will
was going to law school in New Haven in the fall, and
Martha and I would stay in New York. I'm staying because
of you, she said.

I began having physical symptoms. Not being able to
see was one, the main one:

> I lie on the couch but my head is propped on my
> arms. Walking down 5th Avenue I think how pleas-
> ant, what relief, to lie on the couch. As I approach,
> the feeling fades: all too soon, I will have to get up,
> go out the door; the couch turns uncomfortable, un-
> comforting; I must hold myself after all. I see him
> coming toward me down 68th Street, and suddenly
> he is a stranger; I do not know this man, who is he
> . . . Hesitant, I lie down, but I do not look at him. It's
> all in your eyes, these days. No wonder I could not
> see: I did not want to take anything in, he was bad,
> the entire world gone sour. But the world is sour. I
> am standing half in that office and half outside, a
> giant straddling the windowsill. Where am I? I hold
> with my eyes, I reject with my eyes.

Another symptom was an intense physical nervous-
ness. Another was a feeling of falling: the doctor said it was
because I was allowing myself to trust someone else and
was terrified. My mother had been staying with me in New
York; I wanted her to be with me all the time.

> On one of the days of the weekend I went driving
> first with my mother, then with my father, and though
> I always like to arrive, I like the traveling better, the
> being nowhere, not even in control.

Again I prepared for the doctor's vacation:

> I have been cutting him off, cutting him out; wanting
> to have control over his leaving me . . . His face is
> slipping farther and farther away from me; I want to
> cry out, to hold it, grasp at it, at him, not to go away.
> But I no longer know him, who he is, and the words
> are empty, they do not sound in the dim room.

When the doctor went away, my mother came to live with
me.

> I am a big waste of flesh, a retarded child who is
> physically developed but mentally deficient, back-
> ward.

> I am rolling and need the doctor to make me stop; to
> catch me, perhaps, before I roll off the edge of the
> cliff, or start going down the hill so fast that I cannot
> be stopped. Hold my head, one of you, mother or
> doctor, you are a confusion to me.

In the last family session before he left, he had said,
You have found your mother. And I think I have: sometimes
embodied in him; sometimes it's she herself.

o

## A Body Self

### (Dr. Nakhla)

When Grace was discharged from the hospital
in December 1975, she went to live with her sister Martha
and Martha's boyfriend, Will. I was uncertain about how
the new living arrangement would work out and suggested
that we and Martha and Will meet in weekly family ses-

sions. There was a sense of relief for everyone involved (including me, of course). Grace seemed to welcome this background of safety, this structure, but she also felt the loss of her private life of blood, pain, and diary writing, the only world in which she was connected to real and alive feelings.

Grace spent some weekends with her parents, who lived in the country, about an hour and a half from New York. The wrist-cutting incident that occurred in early April 1976 seemed to mark a turning point in Grace's relationship with her mother. Grace had been scalded accidentally by hot water from a faucet, and her mother, while comforting her, remarked on her overreaction. Grace ran out of the house and into a nearby field, where she inflicted a deep cut on her wrist, severing the tendons. Her father met her running back home, terrified and bewildered, and took her to the hospital.

Grace told me about this incident in our next session; one of her first and most significant comments was "You would have been proud of me. I refused to be in control and just screamed and screamed in the hospital." She felt good about her mother's spending the night in the hospital with her; it was the first time that she had taken the risk of turning to her with her rage and destructiveness.

The parents subsequently joined the weekly family sessions. In these sessions, Grace was able to begin to be more open and to convey to her family her feelings of not being alive and real. Once, confronting her mother with those feelings, she pointed to her cut wrist and emphatically stated, "This is real." During Grace's second hospitalization, the family had come to realize the extent of her tormented and isolated existence and self-mutilations. I had been alone in that world with her, but now the family, especially the mother, was sharing it with me. Grace said, "I am spreading my blood."

During the five-month period from April to September 1976, Grace turned to her mother with increasingly regressive and dependent behavior. The mother seemed to accommodate this quite naturally and with devotion. She did not need to tell me what she was going through or ask me for advice or reassurance about how to handle Grace, and she never called me between the family sessions. In one session she did ask Grace to say how she should behave with her. Grace simply responded, "I cannot tell you that. You just have to do it yourself."

Describing a weekend with her parents early in this period, Grace told me of feeling like a little child continuously watched over by her mother. She now spent all weekends at her parents'; her father would readily give up his bed when Grace needed to sleep next to her mother, and her mother often accompanied her back to the city, to her job, on Monday mornings. It was in the context of this merged relationship with her mother that Grace went through certain physically regressive states, such as not being able to see or having blurry vision. Once, however, she said that while walking on familiar streets with her mother she had experienced her surroundings vividly, as though she were seeing things for the first time.

Grace was increasingly aware of and able to tell me about her need for physical closeness to her mother, but she also struggled with it. She knew how to express it only indirectly, by doing something with her mother, such as gardening, and she felt anxious when there was a discontinuity in this closeness. She was frightened when she saw her mother leave at the end of the weekend; similarly, she feared that her mother sleeping next to her in the bed might be dead. And she questioned whether the feeling of closeness was genuine or was just something she was putting on.

In marked contrast to feeling safe and protected in her mother's presence, in my office Grace was usually fearful and detached. At times, she seemed to defend against the feelings of fragmentation and losing control of her violence by holding herself: she would become very still and lie flat on the floor for extended periods. When these anxieties were heightened, she would stand with body and face glued to the wall, as though she were trying to hide or bury herself in it. At other times, she felt claustrophobic, trapped in my room, and she would pace or hit her fist against the window. Sometimes she seemed to feel entombed in her own body and would want to shriek, but the sounds were always muffled and controlled. Or her skin would give her the feeling of being trapped, and she would have the urge to cut herself. When she was most overwhelmed and agitated, she was frightened by impulses to kill herself or kill me.

It was not easy for me to grasp the reason for these shifts—between the terror of noncontainment, of going to pieces, and the terror of being trapped—or, correspondingly, to know how Grace needed me to behave. She might feel comforted by my being physically close or putting my arm around her, or she might be afraid of me and not want me to get near her. On several occasions, she lay still on the couch with her eyes riveted on me. I felt that she was trying to hold me with her eyes, even though they appeared glazed and unfocused. (Later, she described how, when leaving my office in a frightened and fragmented state, she needed to fix her gaze on the traffic lights as she walked.)

I recognized (though I did not interpret this to Grace) the distinction between Grace's feelings of safety and closeness with her mother and her feelings of fearfulness with me as a splitting of the mother into good and bad part-objects. Much later, I came to see her primitive feelings and forms of relatedness in terms of unstable states of separateness and fusion. In her mother's presence, Grace felt merged, but she became anxious when she sensed a discontinuity or became aware of being separate. In contrast, her objective perception of me and the distinct boundaries of the sessions underscored our separateness and the fact that I was not under her control. On the other hand, when she was away from me she unconsciously experienced herself as part of me, within a common boundary: she felt united with me as a "subjective object" (for example, by following in her mind my whereabouts during the day or by figuring out, from where my car was parked, the route I had taken in the morning from my house to my office).[1]

As a result of these unstable states of separateness and fusion, Grace experienced intense conflict between the fear of abandonment and the fear of or wish for merger. Modell (1984a) points out that it is a formidable challenge to the clinician's intuitive skills to judge whether at a given moment the patient needs to be found or fears the doctor's intrusion. Rey (1979) refers to this struggle as the schizoid's "claustrophobic-agoraphobic dilemma." Similarly, Guntrip (1968) describes the schizoid individual's retreat from objects as the "in and out" program; that is, he can be neither in a relationship with another person nor out of it without risking in various ways the loss of his object and himself. The earliest failures for Grace of the "environmental mother" of infancy were sufficiently corrected in this state of merger, both in the analytic situation and in her experiences with her mother, so that a renewed healthy development of psychic structures was gradually evolving. She had moved beyond the sense of fragmentation and the ever-

1. Winnicott used the term "subjective object" to mean "the first object *not yet repudiated as a not-me phenomenon*" (1971a, p. 80); that is, the object of the mother-infant unit, which is indistinguishable from the self and is within the infant's experience of omnipotence. He contrasted that with the later "object objectively perceived."

present threat of annihilation to a sense of aliveness and boundedness of a body self. Various analysts have written about the theoretical and clinical aspects of this process. Relevant to it is Winnicott's application of the concept of the subjective object to (1) the importance of the experiences of omnipotence in ego integration (1962, p. 57); (2) the emerging sense of self, which is initially based on a sense of "being" in contrast to "doing or being done to" (1971a, pp. 72–85); and (3) the existence in health of a private core of the self that is *"isolated, permanently noncommunicating, permanently unknown, in fact unfound"* (1963b, p. 187). Stern's (1985) ideas on the development of a sense of a "core self" are also pertinent. He based that sense of a physical or body self on the integration of the self experiences of self-agency, self-coherence, self-affectivity, and self-history.

E. Gaddini (1982) terms the earliest mental representations of the body self, the visual images of the integrated and separate self, "fantasies on the body." He states that these images are usually inanimate and round-shaped. Grace had used the images of an empty bottle and a long tunnel with a light at the end to describe herself. She conveyed her vague sense of body image in describing to me how when she got dressed in the morning she had the feeling of not knowing what it was like to dress herself, of not knowing what to do or how to do it.

Gaddini uses the term "fantasies in the body" to refer to the primitive mental experiences of the body that precede "fantasies on the body," and describes these as fantasies of the nonintegrated self related to specific bodily functions and sensations. They remain enclosed in a primitive and exclusive body-mind-body circuit and are not available to further mental elaboration. Mahler (1968, pp. 11–12) similarly emphasizes the major shift of the libidinal cathexis from the inside of the body toward the periphery of the body as a major step in the development of a body ego and a body image. She states that another parallel step is the ejection of destructive unneutralized aggressive energy beyond the body-self boundaries. Grace's earlier mental experiences of her body were of a painful, bloody physical fragmentation of her body parts and body limits: "I don't just break a bottle, I smash it again and again into splinters with my arms, wrist, hand."

Gaddini (1982, 1987) develops Greenacre's (1958a, 1958b) term "psychophysical syndromes" for the psychopathology within this primitive body-mind-body circuit, which is a defense against the threat of annihilation (see also McDougall 1989, chap. 1). Grace's repeated wrist scratches and cuts can be regarded as a psychophysical syndrome that insured her survival: "As the marks disappeared, I felt I had to make new ones, to keep myself alive." Mahler (1968) and Mahler and McDevitt (1982, p. 833) in their work with psychotic children have discussed autoaggressive activity as an attempt to define body-self boundaries and an attempt to "feel alive." Grace's sense of boundedness in preserving her "continuity of being" was, of course, also developed by internalizing the physical sensations connected with the care of her wounds and all the other aspects of "holding" (R. Gaddini 1987).[2]

Grace was curious about the anatomy of her wrists and the surgical repair of them. Once when she was examining with fascination a cut on her wrist, with its beads of subcutaneous tissue, she said to me, "It looks like a mouth with teeth. Do you see them?" This represents a further development of her body scheme, through an awareness of

2. See Winnicott's holding and handling (1960a) and mirror role of the mother (1971d); Mahler and McDevitt (1982, pp. 833, 837) on the importance of the sensations perceived from the caregiver/libidinal object; Adler's (1985) idea of "holding introjects"; and Tolpin's (1971) concept of "transmuting internalizations."

inner feelings connected to her oral impulses, and, possibly, a communication of her devouring and dangerously active oral-sadistic libidinal needs. Understandably, doctors who attended to the wounds dismissed or were troubled by her desire to watch and to ask questions about the surgery. She learned not to draw attention to herself in emergency rooms, however, in order to avoid being questioned about the scars on her wrists or having to undergo a psychiatric examination. I became acquainted with a plastic surgeon, Dr. V., who was quite accessible, and accepting of Grace's situation and behavior, and with whom she felt at ease. She went to him for the follow-up care of her severed tendons; at the same time, seemingly more comfortable with the exploration of her body, she got an old copy of an anatomy textbook.

A final comment concerns Grace's sense of bodily separateness and the creation of a transitional object. The finger painting made with her blood (and, later, a vial filled with her blood that she gave me to "add to my collection") could be viewed as a creation symbolic of the illusion of our unity.[3] Kafka (1969), in his paper "The Body as a Transitional Object: A Psychoanalytic Study of a Self-Mutilating Patient," proposes the idea that part of the body (blood in the case of his patient) representing the internalized mother can be a transitional object.[4] I think that R. Gaddini's (1978, 1987) term "precursor" (of a transitional object) is more correct. Winnicott (1971a) in the introduction to "Playing and Reality" draws attention to Gaddini's studies of transitional phenomena and says that he also finds value in her idea of precursors.

3. A similarity may be drawn to the smearing of feces, as seen in some severely regressed patients (see, for example, Barnes and Berke, 1971).

4. Searles (1979a, pp. 570–72) reviews this paper as it relates to the analyst's feeling-participation in such a therapeutic symbiosis.

My four-week vacation in August 1976 marked the peak
of Grace's regressive dependence on her mother and of the
threat of a regressive breakdown. Grace worked for the first
and last weeks of my vacation, and her mother stayed with
her in the city. She also spent a week with her parents in
Maine (where she had spent vacations as a child) and a
week at their house. At the end of each of the weeks with
her parents Grace felt anxious about the disruption of what
she described as an experience of a continuous, carefree
closeness with her mother and father. I spoke to her weekly
on the telephone, and on the last weekend she told me that
she had become extremely anxious and had developed a
serious blurring of vision.

Grace came to her first session after my vacation accompanied by her mother. She appeared tense and rigid and
said that she couldn't see clearly and felt too sick to continue working. She and her mother had discussed the possibility of her quitting her job. We agreed that she would
not go to work for the next two days and would have her
eyes examined; I would then arrange for a more extended
medical leave of absence. (Except for the two hospitaliza-
tions, this was the only time she missed work during the
entire treatment.) Two days later, Grace was feeling better
and was able to see. She and her mother had decided that
she would return to work but live with her parents and
commute to New York. At the end of the week, Grace again
came to her session with her mother, but this time she came
into my office alone. She was controlled and detached and
told me that she had decided to continue to live with her
sister and to spend only weekends with her parents.

Grace's attachment to her mother seemed to be rapidly
dissolving, and this development brought on anxieties and
conflicts as she moved toward a greater sense of separateness.

# 7
# Finding a Self

(September–December 1976)

o

## Surviving Alone

**(Grace Jackson)**

Suddenly I lost my sense of my mother; suddenly, I thought, I don't know where we are anymore. I had somehow cut myself off from the safety of her. I am not small, hiding myself in her warmth: yet still I did not feel able to take care of myself.

Maybe I didn't want to give up my adult self after all. And the eye anxiousness had got better. I went to meet my family and the doctor feeling cold and self-contained from my day at work. They were all aware of my distance:

The old holding of myself. It is not so easy to drop it. I do not want to be touched, for I am safe in my containment. My container: I am in a box, and you are all standing around gaping. What can you do? I keep you all away.

I suppose that having found my mother I was now separating from her. I suppose my mother was something around which to center myself during the summer; but then something changed—I could not live my life as part of my mother, which was what I was beginning to do. That was the engulfing, smothering feeling. "But I move out on my own and become terrified. Am I terrified? Or am I making that up, too . . . With my parents I am in a padded nest, silent and safe."

I felt that they were taking away my self, my private inner self: I raged at them and at the doctor. I hated and avoided them. I was tired of being the focus of my family. I felt that I was again being the "good" child, complying with what they wanted, and I was afraid of being taken over, suffocated by them.

My things were arranged in the bedroom in my sister's apartment—now I had a room. Still I didn't feel that it was my house, although Will was in New Haven and Martha went back and forth a lot. In this apartment all I wanted to do was read novels and watch TV. The ugliness and clutter of the place reflected my state of mind, which I wanted to escape from, did not want to look at. I was happy to have my typewriter, yet I found writing difficult—I felt myself on the surface: of words, of life. I insisted on having time alone, and stopped spending every weekend at my parents'. I had to write, but I was writing the same self-analysis over and over, the fight between self and family, feelings and fear: what am I feeling, am I feeling anything: "Everything washes around and through me as if I were a shadow."

In the summer I had started swimming. I joined the Y near my office and went swimming either on my lunch hour or before work. I was held by the water; I was calm; even free. The water takes away the burden of the body. (Is that having a body or not?) I wanted to be left alone, by my mother, by my sister; even by the doctor. My mother—despite everything—in her anxiety is saying, I just don't understand; you have everything; you have no real worries: what is the matter? If only you were more interested in your job. The doctor: who, what is he? You are like a disease, I tell him, that I carry inside me and tell no one about; I go on with my daily life, but I am being destroyed inside. He says this is reliving what I went through as a child: the internalizing of my mother. The fear of destroying her and the world. I sit again on the floor, keeping a distance from him. I feel safer there, that he cannot get to me . . . and yet he is inside me, controlling me. He and my mother. He as my mother . . . The razor blades, the bottles are always before me, but I have forgotten what they signify, and so my hands are still.

Martha was fed up. She said she was going to leave New York—she wasn't doing anything for me and felt it was impossible that she could. We hardly spoke, though we were living in the same house.

The doctor and I talk about how I destroy my experiences, turning the good to bad, feeling good things as if they had happened to someone else. You have not been held long enough, he says. You want the session to go on until you are ready to end it. As a crying child clings to its mother until it is ready to move away. But I clung to my mother and then moved away: and was I ready? It doesn't seem so. The will to destruction fights the instinct to survive. In cutting off the destructive feelings, I cut off the loving feelings, too. I am empty, soulless. I type and type and get nowhere. I think and think: the same.

The doctor's imperturbability makes him inhuman: I can talk of killing him without fear. But that is not really accurate. If I can talk about destroying him without fear there is the implication that he does not believe me. Then I have to cut to show him. I did imagine beating him, strangling him; I felt my hands around his soft neck.

The typewriter, in a way, represents a loss of hope; a failure:

> The pages fill slowly and crazily, words from here and there, overlapping, repeating, contradicting. I think I need all my sentences about tea and cigarettes and what music is playing for some sort of anchor, to keep me going. Though it is merely a kind of chatter. And over all looms the face, the voice of the doctor; in the background a ghostly muttering chorus of the family.

The doctor went to London for Christmas: I am envious, sort of: would like to go there myself. I tried to imagine him there. Thinking about him makes him vanish: if he goes, there are only the shaky external things to hold on to.

o

## A Separate Self

### (Dr. Nakhla)

After the summer vacation, Grace abruptly broke away from the deep regression and dependence on her mother.[1] She turned to me as a "substitute mother,"

1. Mahler and her co-workers (1975) outline the intrapsychic separation process in the developing infant and small child as running along the track of differentiation, distancing, boundary-structuring, and disengagement from the mother.

only to find that she did not know me and had lost any sense of the connection between us. During the next four months, she continued the struggle to separate herself from her family, experiencing feelings of loss, isolation, and rage. These gradually intensified, and came to a peak at another break in treatment, around Christmas, when I left for a two-week vacation in England.

Grace described herself as "boxed in," or "in a bubble," cut off from me. She was usually quiet and detached, looking away from me, with her hair down over her face. This state of unrelatedness resembles Modell's (1968, 1976) description of the "cocoon transference"; the patient feels encased in a "plastic bubble" or a cocoon, and attempts to maintain an illusion of self-sufficiency. Guntrip (1968) has reported this cutoff feeling as being like a plate-glass window between the patient and the world. Grace was able, however, to communicate that she felt lost and sad, and a number of times she expressed this by crying, something she had not done before. She reported dreams of being abandoned by me:

> I am too busy to continue seeing her and refer her to another doctor.
>
> I react to an outburst of her anger by leaving her.
>
> I am at the top of a mountain and she is unable to reach me.

Grace continued to spend most weekends at her parents', but in the weekly family sessions her mother and sister said that they were worried: they were angry or felt helpless at her detachment. At a session after Grace had spent two consecutive weekends alone, she became enraged when her parents asked about what she had done, resenting the fact that she was the focus of the family's questions and attention. Nevertheless, she was able to explain that although being alone had been difficult and she had missed them, she needed to be on her own, to feel that she was a person and not just a good child attached to them. Grace said to me that it seemed futile to try to be separate and herself with her family, since her mother was always aware of how distressed Grace really felt.

Grace's father seemed to accept her desire for independence and suggested that she feel free to discuss or ask questions about whatever she wanted. Her mother, on the other hand, was afraid that Grace might be doing what she had done as a child, cutting herself off "without taking that Mommy feeling with her" and again becoming cold and aloof, not alive. She still feared that Grace might kill herself, and after finding some broken glass in Grace's apartment, she discussed, in a family session, her feelings of frustration about the treatment and suggested that Grace leave New York. Grace acknowledged that she, too, felt a sense of despair but asserted that she wanted to continue the treatment, even though she could not explain or justify it. I was relieved and gratified that the mother quickly accepted, and supported, Grace's decision. Her father responded that there was no choice but to continue the treatment.

Still, the family sessions were tense, with Grace openly resenting them. The mother, however, said that she needed them to maintain contact and to help her deal with her own anxieties about Grace. In spite of Grace's feelings and conflict, I, too, felt the need for the support and involvement of the family. For Grace, the focus on her sickness in the family was another form of being taken away from herself and made responsible for them, just as she had been as a child, by being good and compliant.[2] She seemed to

2. Modell, in "On Having the Right to a Life" (1984b) and "Self-Psychology as a Psychology of Conflict" (1984c), discusses the feeling of guilt and disloyalty in the process of individuation and in

make a breakthrough in the struggle to be separate when, taking up her father's suggestion that she should feel free to talk about anything, she confronted the family with her father's drinking and his feelings of depression. To my surprise, he readily talked about his own long struggle with a sense of failure, saying that in the past he had even had thoughts of suicide. Martha, who had become discouraged by Grace's distance and resigned to the fact that she was not making a difference in her life ("I am sick of Grace's sickness"), said that she, too, felt at a loss about her life and seemed to fall back on the fact that she would end up getting married to Will. During the next session, the father, on his own initiative, talked about his family and childhood. A sister, five years older than he, had died in a flu epidemic just after his birth, and he had grown up as an indulged only child. As a young man he had been "wild," and he had not finished college. He felt that he was a failure and a disappointment to his father, a lawyer, who loved books, and also music, especially as his sight failed and he could no longer read. But with his marriage and the birth of his children "all was forgiven." This was the first family session in which Grace was not the center of attention and in which I learned details of her family background.

In the individual sessions, however, Grace's sense of frustration and isolation escalated. The world felt "painful," and she could not take anything in: "Everything feels

---

having a separate life and separate fate from that of other family members. Also, Searles, in "Phases of a Patient-Therapist Interaction in the Psychotherapy of Chronic Schizophrenia" (1961), describes several issues in the phase of resolution of the symbiosis that are pertinent to this account, such as allowing the patient to take responsibility for his illness and his life in the face of threats of suicide, psychotic decompensation, the patient's guilt about being a separate person, reactions to the loss of symbiotic gratification to family members, and threats of the breakup of the treatment.

like I am touching a snake," or "licking dirt off the floor." She felt that she was under my all-powerful control and at a confused standstill, and was terrified and guilty that her actions would be destructive to me and to her family.[3]

Grace became more agitated and violent. Sometimes she would pace menacingly around the office, clutching my metal letter opener or a glass ashtray; once she was overcome by the fear that I and the whole room were disappearing, and she hid in a corner behind a chair. She brought a paper bag of bottles to a session and told me that she could have smashed the windshield of my car. She told me that she did smash glass sometimes in her apartment and on the street, and that walking on crowded sidewalks she would purposely collide with people.

In addition to her terror and anger, she had intense feelings of sadness and loss. She often sobbed in her sessions: "I used to have a facade but now I have nothing." Even her diary writing had lost its meaning. She reported a dream in which I was kissing her good-bye through a pane of glass. She felt there was always a wall between us. She described me as "a stranger, and every time you are a different stranger."

In another dream she was going into and out of a subway station, unable to find her way to the train, until finally she collapsed, sobbing. This was reenacted between us several times during the weeks before my Christmas vacation, when Grace became overwhelmed at leaving my office at the end of the session. Once after she had left, I heard her crying and screaming on the street. I found her in the middle of a stack of garbage bags piled on the edge of the

---

3. The role of aggression and destructiveness in emotional development has been discussed by several writers, including Winnicott (1950, 1963a, 1969b), Mahler (1971, p. 412), and Searles (1966–67, pp. 60–66).

sidewalk and brought her back inside. A short while later, two police officers, responding to calls from neighbors, came into my office and questioned both of us. Distraught, she lay on the floor, crying quietly. After the police left, I sat on the floor and comforted her until she was able to leave, two hours later. (This was the only occurrence of an extended office session.) Grace had found that riding the subways and being driven in a car had a soothing effect, similar to the sensations described in her diary concerning "tea and cigarettes and what music is playing," sentences she experienced as an "anchor, to keep me going." Ogden (1989), in his formulation of the concept of the autistic-contiguous position, has described such activities as defenses against the primitive anxieties of the disruption of the sense of cohesion and boundedness. When I felt that she was too frightened to leave at the end of a session, I would drive her to the subway station two blocks away, which seemed to comfort her, and ask that she call me when she got home.

Because of my apprehension about leaving Grace during my Christmas vacation (particularly since she had refused to spend any of the time with her parents), I suggested the possibility of her going to the hospital. Although she acknowledged my concern and expressed some guilt, she was angry: I was controlling her, retaliating for the way she had been behaving, destroying her. "Why are you doing this to me?" "I feel that you have a knife and are going to cut me." In her last session before my trip, Grace was distressed and agitated, and at the end needed me to take her to the subway. The following morning, there was a family session, at which Grace's mother again expressed her fear of Grace's being alone. She had been awakened that morning by a dream in which Grace was screaming for her. As the session progressed, however, Grace surprisingly began to speak of her good feelings of connection to her father, recalling the two previous family sessions, during which the father had talked about himself and his father. She also mentioned how her father had helped her move out of the apartment she and Susan had shared and how they had had lunch together afterward. She linked these with other warm and loving feelings and memories: toward her grandfather (her father's father, to whom she had always felt close) and toward the psychoanalyst who had interviewed her during her second hospitalization and had reminded her of her grandfather.[4] She was afraid that my leaving would interrupt and cut her off from these good feelings.

At the end of the session Grace asked to see me alone. In a genuinely loving and tender way she told me that she did not want to part with angry and violent feelings. I was relieved and hugged her, reassuring her that I would be fine and would see her in two weeks.

4. On the role of the father in the separation-individuation process, see Abelin (1971); and Mahler's (1971, p. 416) "impressions" concerning the role of the pre-oedipal father as protector from the potentially overwhelming "mother of separation."

# 8
# A Self
# and Others

○

## The Beginnings of an Individual Identity

### (Dr. Nakhla)

In our first session after my return, Grace acknowledged that she had missed me and had felt anxious at the awareness of her loving feelings toward me. I had promised to send her a postcard, and each day she had looked forward to its arrival, while at the same time trying not to. (In fact, she received it the day of my return; it was a map of the London Underground system.) In the next session, she elaborated on her positive feelings and spoke about her fear that they would be lost when she actually saw me. She also told me that there was a man at her office,

John, "who seems to like me." She had gone out with him a few times, and had enjoyed it, but because it was an experience she had not had for a long time she found it strange and confusing. She didn't know if her good feelings were related to him or to me. She said she felt comfortable with him; she liked the physical closeness, and liked listening to him talk, especially as he was focused on things outside of himself and was not introspective. She again expressed the fear of losing the good feelings and experiences, attributing this to her tendency to keep them to herself and not talk about them. (Later she told me that she had forced herself to talk to me about John, determined not to let him "go the way of other things, not to keep him a shadowy nonexistence in the life I live with the doctor.")

A week later, Grace's sister Eleanor came from the West Coast to visit her family for a month. Grace was anxious about seeing Eleanor, and she had a dream in which Eleanor had a beautiful face and she was unable to look at her. It reminded her of the dream she had had in which she feared she would turn to stone if she looked at Eleanor's face; her first analyst, Dr. P., had associated this to the Greek myth of Medusa.[1]

Grace talked about how she had always been protective of her sister. Eleanor was the one who could cry or be angry or even hit Grace without her resisting or objecting. Grace

1. Laing (1960) discusses at some length the notion of petrification of self or other in connection with overwhelming threats to one's sense of realness and identity. Wright (1991) refers to Medusa in his chapter "The Other's View," in which he discusses the negative subjective feelings derived from the experience of being looked at. Arvanitakis (1987) uses the myth of Perseus and Medusa to develop his model of the significance of the analytic frame in the treatment of archaic anxieties that can be contained and transformed into tolerable images. It was the interposed reflecting shield-mirror that enabled Perseus to deal with his terrifying monster.

had been more successful in school but felt she would have given that up to have Eleanor succeed. I suggested to Grace that perhaps her life had been interrupted by—sacrificed to—Eleanor at a very early time, with her mother's pregnancy and Eleanor's birth, and that she had never acknowledged the rage she must feel. The Medusa dreams were interpreted both as Grace's own life having turned to stone, having been brought to a standstill, and as her being "petrified" to look at Eleanor's face and see someone she had destroyed.

Eleanor and Martha came to several sessions. Grace and Eleanor spoke of how they had attempted to be free—of the family and of each other—and to find themselves by moving away: Eleanor to the West Coast, Grace to England. They acknowledged that the physical distance between them was also a protection against the fear and guilt produced by knowing of any pain or unhappiness in the other's life. Martha said that a few days earlier she, Grace, and Eleanor had stayed up all night talking about their childhood; she had been relieved and pleased by Grace's involvement in the discussion. They seemed to be continuing their conversation in my office, and in the course of it I learned that Eleanor and Martha had resented Grace and teased her because she was always good.

Grace and Eleanor complained about the constant intrusions when they were growing up, with their parents' friends "dropping by as though the house were their local pub." They were taken away from their own activities to socialize with family friends. Eleanor said she had vowed that when she had her own house she would have there only the people she really wanted. In a subsequent session they confronted their mother with these feelings about the lack of privacy. She responded by talking about her own childhood: she had grown up in a small city in Maine, not just an only child but the only grandchild of two large families. As the focus of many adults, she was spoiled and sheltered, and her relatives, especially on her mother's side, laid much emphasis on the importance of the family. She was glad to go to college and get away from a life she had experienced as isolating and stifling. When she got married, she determined that she would have "an open house, with no closed doors," a free and outgoing environment, such as she felt she had missed. She realized now that in attempting to correct her own life she had hurt her children.

Eleanor's visit and the family sessions enabled the sisters to feel closer and also to acknowledge one another as individuals. In March, Eleanor got married; Martha, who was also planning to get married, decided to move to New Haven to live with Will. Grace was happy for her sisters and felt that she no longer had to be responsible for them. Yet in many ways she still perceived herself as the focus of the family—she was still, as she put it, "the child who represents the family's problems yet who is supposed to make them go away: 'If she's all right we don't have to think about ourselves—as a family—anymore.'" Her mother, she said, made her feel like the child she "was trying so hard not to be: the one who needs to be watched, taken care of." The family also seemed to disrupt the relationship between her and me, in which she could get something for herself; and she again pressed me to end the family sessions. Her mother felt that Grace was becoming more connected to and comfortable with the family, and although she no longer feared for her physical safety she did worry about whether Grace would continue to get well and maintain that closeness. I, too, had become less worried about Grace, and we talked about ending the family sessions. Grace reported a dream that brought into focus her struggle and her need for the sessions to end:

There is a family session and we are to meet somewhere else, a conference room in a building near the United Nations. Grace thinks she and her parents are going to arrive there separately, but suddenly they are at her house, and she is annoyed. They are late. She is trying to get them going and is afraid they will be late and I will not wait. They seem to delay and delay. At her house she watches the minutes ticking by on the clock. Her parents leave or disappear. She gets to this place and looks everywhere for me but cannot find me. I have not waited. She is furious with her parents and wakes up with the sense that I am dead.

Although Grace was eager to be separate, now that Martha was moving away, and began enthusiastically to look for an apartment, she was afraid of having her own, individual life. This was expressed in the next few weeks as she became more distressed, fearing the loss of her connection to me. She reported a dream: "Someone is handing out presents, puts something in my hand. It is an old nail." She then told me that one day long ago she had in fact picked up a nail on the street and had carried it in her pocket or in her purse. She took it out at work one day and it had been lying beside her typewriter. Seeing it made her remember the dream. I pointed out to Grace her intense anxiety about the sense of separateness. The nail, I suggested, was symbolic of the link between us and would keep us in a united state, warding off separateness and the fear of death.

She subsequently told me the following dream (from Grace's diary):

I am at the doctor's office. I wait and wait. He finally comes, wearing checked pants and a shiny

green jacket. He mumbles something about why he is
late; carrying a bag, as if to play golf. You see I don't
have to go to work today. You should have told me, I
say; I don't have to go either, we could have made the
time later. Lengthy explanation of why it is important
to keep times the same. Then it is his house, I see his
wife—pale blond woman, soft face, wearing a bathrobe. They go together, I think. Scene of me standing
outside the window, head resting on sill. Then my
head on hers, then doctor's on mine. They have been
eating breakfast: eggs, bacon, a large fish, potatoes.
Sense of her asking if I want some, which I refuse. He
eats some potatoes. He is also standing outside. Inter-
spersed with scenes of him in his office. (Now he too
seems to be wearing a bathrobe.) He sits in my chair,
which is in front of the window. Three young women
in bathrobes (sometimes more) dance around him,
climb on him; i.e., sit on his lap. This scene recurs. I
go back to his house, his wife, who is kind. Many
people: they are having a party, or are about to. Pink
tablecloths outside on the lawn. I see a woman from
my office in a pink satin shirt leaning out of a window. I ask her why she is there. It's some sort of international (students?) gathering. They invited a certain number of journalists, she says. Why don't you
come too. I am here for a different reason, I say; she
seems to know what this is. Return to dr, tell him I
am going to go to his party. Another lengthy explanation about mixing business with social life, how it
cannot, must not, be done. I argue (or try to) a little
(perhaps a lot: sense of antagonism?). Then he walks
away, down a hill, up a hill that is the front yard of
the farm [her parents' house], toward the plane tree
with the swing, and I follow, thinking to be alone
with him at last. I pick up a heavy wooden disk and

throw it at him, aiming so it will not hit but fall beside him. But it ricochets up and strikes him in the shoulder. He falls? I rush over to him, then it is I who am lying on the ground, in tears, saying very sadly, You can go away now, I have finally hurt you, irreparably, unforgivably. You can go away now. And my crying wakes me up.

Interpreting the dream, I pointed out to Grace that it showed her devouring impulses and sexual excitement, and how she is overcome by guilt and collapses into despair because her rage at my rejection and frustration of her wishes has finally destroyed me. There are indications of the development of the capacity for concern (Winnicott 1963a): taking responsibility for instinctual impulses and perceiving the object as a whole and real person. (These ideas are also tied in with Winnicott's concept of the "use of an object.") The capacity for concern is comparable to the concepts of depressive anxieties, guilt, and reparation in the Kleinian depressive position.

The oedipal material in the dream, which was not interpreted, represents what Guntrip (1968, p. 45) has described as an earlier pathological oedipal complex, in which the parents are unreal and idealized. The child will turn from mother to father, going back and forth between them, in his quest for a secure, stable, loving environment. Conversely, it may represent Chasseguet-Smirgel's (1986, pp. 74–91) hypothesis of the archaic matrix of the oedipus complex: a primary desire to discover a universe without obstacles, identified with the mother's belly, which is stripped of its contents, and to which one has free access, thereby recovering a state of unfettered pleasure. There is an equivalent fantasy of destroying reality that is represented by the father, his penis, and the children—the contents and obstacles in the mother's belly. Chasseguet-Smirgel (1992) develops these ideas by defining the paternal *function*, the obstacle between mother and infant, as being of fundamental importance in the early development of the human mind.[2] She further hypothesized that there is a correspondence between the psychoanalytic situation and the structure of the mental apparatus. The analytic situation is viewed as an enclave wherein the basic human wish of a regression against the uterine maternal matrix can be experienced in the content of the session, whereas the fixed structural frame of the session, which it is the analyst's task to preserve, indicates that this relationship must be relinquished.

The dream was in a sense reenacted the following day. Grace arrived at her early-morning session appearing disturbed and detached, and I could see that she had cut her wrist. She said she had gone to bed the night before feeling isolated and cold. (In fact, she had had no heat or hot water in her apartment for two days.) Overwhelmed by feelings of coldness and deadness as she lay on the floor (where she often slept), she had cut her wrist and, with a sense of calm and relief, watched the blood drip into a vial: "It was all done in cold blood." As she walked behind me into the office that morning she had had the impulse to throw the vial at me. During the session Grace remained withdrawn and refused to show me the cut, saying that she would go to an emergency room in the evening after work. I nonetheless phoned Dr. V., the plastic surgeon, and drove her to his office. I was going to drop her off, as I had done in the past, but this time, to my surprise, she asked me to come in and stay with her. I had never been with her while she was having a cut attended to. In her diary she wrote:

2. This paternal *function* bears a similarity to Winnicott's (1951) notion of the maternal task of "graduated disillusionment and graduated failure" of her infant.

Dr. V. the magician. He is on one side of me stitching,
the doctor is on the other holding my hand and my
head. The stitched wrist hurts. I feel the holes in the
skin through which the little fish hook drew the
thread. What a fascination is in these threads. Do they
really tie me to the doctor? I must hold in my mind
the memory of being safe between the two doctors:
it's the dream, my head is on the windowsill between
the heads of the doctor and his wife.

Grace called me that evening, as planned. She was
feeling terrible; her apartment was a mess and still lacked
heat and hot water. She said there was no one she could
go to for a hot bath. Again, she seemed to be turning to me
from her aloneness and her cold world with the wish to be
in my warm house.

This change in her behavior brought to mind Winnicott's (1969b) ideas about the "use of an object": I had
survived her destruction. Consequently, she was able to
perceive me as a real and external object and was able to
"use" me.

○

## One World and Two Separate Worlds

**(Dr. Nakhla)**

Grace talked about feeling alone and cut off
from me. We are in two separate worlds, she said; longingly
she spoke of cutting as a relief from that feeling. The first
moments of cutting and bleeding, she said, gave her a hard-
to-describe sense of "blissful calm," and although she hated
the destructive consequences, the act was compelling and
difficult to resist. I compared it to a drug, an addiction, and
asked if there was anything else that gave her that feeling.

She described staying up all night writing and then seemed to realize that writing could have that effect. I was struck by her comment and recognized with renewed interest the importance of her diary. I suggested that I see the diary. Grace smiled: it would be impossible, since there were fifteen large volumes. I immediately offered to go to her house to see them. She was surprised and excited by the idea. In the next session she told me that she had had to write it down in order to believe it; similarly, she said, as a child she could not believe a day had existed unless she wrote about it.

Although there was a shared excitement in talking about her writing, Grace also was anxious that I might destroy it in some way, as she felt her mother had done. In college, Grace had given her mother a story she had written. Over the years, Grace had written several versions of the story, and her mother's response to this new version was "Can't you write about something else!" I apologized for not having fully understood the significance of the diary before. I had seen the diary writing as a defensive mental activity of her false self (Winnicott, 1960c). Now I realized that although it served that function, I could be overlooking its relation to the creative and imaginative aspects of the self. She had been unable to talk about it because she didn't believe in it strongly enough, fearing that it was meaningless, dead. She explained that as a child she had felt compelled to write down each day, as though something terrible would happen if she didn't. In an attempt to help me understand what her diary, and writing, meant to her, she showed me some quotations from Joan Didion:

> The impulse to write things down is a peculiarly compulsive one, inexplicable to those who do not share it, useful only accidentally, secondarily, in the

way that any compulsion tries to justify itself. I suppose that it begins or does not begin in the cradle. . . .
Keepers of private notebooks are a different breed al-
together, lonely and resistant rearrangers of things,
anxious malcontents, children afflicted apparently at
birth with some presentiment of loss. (Didion 1969,
pp. 132–33)

I began to feel scattered, upset, not myself.

I could have gone for a walk on the beach. Instead, I went to my office and just sat in front of my
typewriter, and it was OK. I got control. I calmed
down. I'm only myself in front of my typewriter.

Sometimes I think I can't think at all unless I'm
behind my typewriter. (Braudy 1977, p. 108)

Grace told me about how she made lists, not only of
things to do but of thoughts, experiences. She would write
them in a notebook that she carried or on scraps of paper.
She showed me a list she had in her bag:

letters—Catherine H, Kare, Uncle George
call M
Anderson Isometrics—maps
S Weil bio
Should I carry a comb?
Does he [Dr. Nakhla] keep notes or records?
View of Central Park from Park Ave., 2 blocks away,
is similar to Hampstead Heath from our apartment.

The ideas in Winnicott's paper "Mind and Its Relation
to the Psyche-Soma" (1949a) are central to understanding
the meaning and experience of Grace's diary writing as a
function of her mind, which had become the location of
her false self.

Winnicott made a distinction between the mind (intellect) and the psyche, which he described in the early developmental context of the self as "the imaginative elaboration of somatic parts, feelings, and functions, that is of physical aliveness." He viewed the earliest phase of individual development as constituting the interrelationship of the soma and the psyche. He believed that "the mind does not exist as an entity in the individual's scheme of things provided the individual psyche-soma or body scheme has come satisfactorily through the very early developmental stages; mind is then no more than a special case of the functioning psyche-soma" (p. 244). Winnicott maintains that in health the mental activity of the infant's mind can make up for the deficiencies of the good-enough mother. In cases of too-early maternal failure or erratic mothering, the mind overreacts, and mental activity becomes a substitute for maternal care.

Grace's precocious intellectual development had been pathological and dissociated from the aliveness of her body and its function; consequently, it had become "an encumbrance to the psyche-soma" and to her continuity of being, which constitutes the self.

Grace had found a new apartment, and she suggested that I wait until she moved to come and see her diary. She was eager to move; she described the apartment to me and drew a floor plan, and then she asked me about my apartment and I drew a plan of it for her. It was the first time she had had a place that felt like her own. She wanted to do everything herself; in particular, she did not want her mother involved. Friends helped her paint, however, and she did let her mother help put down new linoleum in the kitchen.

It was an unusual and exciting experience when I visited Grace's new apartment and, over a cup of tea, looked through her diaries. The diary was impressive: the sheer volume of pages documenting a whole life. It seemed to me, as I told her, that her story was all contained there for her to write one day. I left with a sense of aliveness, of having been with Grace as a real person in her own world. The following week she told me that she was pleased I had come, even though she felt that I was abandoning her when I left. It reminded her of the way she had felt after the session during my summer vacation, two years earlier, when she had experienced an overwhelming sense of a loss of herself and inflicted her first serious wrist cut.

She accepted and valued my recognition of her separateness and her sense of individual identity, but she was anxious about the loss of the underlying unity, even fearing that it had never existed, was unreal, or was just a game that I had been playing. This feeling of unreality persisted; and for two weeks she did not talk about the visit at all.

Then she came to a session appearing distressed and sat on the edge of the couch, silent and cut off. I sat next to her and put my arm around her. She crawled into my body and several times forcefully thrust her head into me, letting out small shrieks. When she became quieter, I said to her that she really wanted to get back inside me, into my womb, where she would again be one with me. She remained calm and quiet, with my hand resting gently on her back, for the rest of the session. Two days later, she reported the following dream:

> I was in a subway station; it was 68th Street [the station for my office]. I was waiting for a train, and then I was on the train, and the doctor was the driver. I didn't really know where I was going. I got off, then thought of going to the end of the line. I tried to look at a map, to see where that was: somehow the subway was the London Underground—maybe it had been

London all along, for the trains came from the opposite direction they would have in New York. The last
stop was called St. Elizabeth Axe or maybe Acts,
which seemed not to be the real end of the line: the
Central line, the red route [on the London Underground map]. The route continued for a long distance
in black, but I knew it was the Central line because it
was going toward Epping. Black on black: it was dark
everywhere. I found myself leaning on the window of
the driver's cab, touching the doctor's arm. He was
the reason I wanted to stay on the train, to stay with
him, while at the same time thinking it was a sort of
ploy, not quite permissible, to be with him always or
for him not to leave me. But I knew he would know
that and might not like it. I then got out of the subway station by a ladder through a hole or passage.
There was a scene in a darkened house, carrying
things up and down stairs, waiting for someone to
come.

I interpreted to Grace that being in the Underground
and in the train with me was again her wish to return to
the womb. The interruption on the Central line (the red—
blood—line), the not continuing to the end, was the trauma
of birth, which left her confused and in a black darkness.
The dream also illustrates the hyperactivity of Grace's intellect in defending against her confusion and anxieties at
being cut off and abandoned. Often when she felt cut off
from me she would ride the subways to contain her terror
and chaos. In the dream I am with her in her world of the
subways as the driver of the train, and in her memory,
helping her to locate herself, is my postcard map of the
London Underground.

The black darkness of separateness, the loss and destruction of our unity, is also the darkness of a birth. Little and Flarsheim (1972) speak of such experiences "as a re-birth and re-creation of the self and of the world. *Birth fantasies and memories in analysis are not traceable only to the actual birth experience. They can come from memory traces of the individual's emergence from the early state of subjective oneness with the mother and entrance into the state of relatedness with separate persons.* In contrast to the single event of physical birth this psychological 'birth experience' can occur repeatedly" (p. 325).[3]

Grace told me that she had never had a houseplant because she feared that she could not keep one alive. For her new apartment, she had bought a geranium; it seemed to be doing well, and she hoped it wouldn't die.

o

## The Diary: Illusion or Reality?

### (Grace Jackson)

The doctor said that when I moved to my new apartment he wanted to come and see it—and see my diaries. I could hardly believe it. Did I even want it? Yet wasn't it what I had often wished to myself? Did he really want to come? How could he? He was going to take part? Write my story with me. He said it himself. "You see me as outside your world, you never experience the feeling of unity: only with glass, razor blades." Now he would enter

---

3. Little (1985, 1990), in her account of her analysis with Winnicott, describes reliving a birth experience. Winnicott, in his paper "Birth Memories, Birth Trauma, and Anxiety" (1949b), asserts that traumatic birth experiences can be literally relived in the analytic situation.

my world: the diary, which he had rejected, dismissed. He would know that hidden self; I had to dare to reveal it.

"I'm sorry," he said, "if that makes sense, that I didn't know sooner, didn't realize, about the diary. There are things that could be said in my defense."

Yes, I didn't tell you; rather, I didn't insist. When you said "This is dead, there is no life in it," I believed you.

I believed him, and yet I had kept on, for at first, of course, there was Susan, and together we believed in writing. But I think she may have begun to see the diary as a kind of sickness, too—she and everyone else. They were all with you, I told him. Not seeing, not realizing the diary is me.

*Is it?*

Maybe he was right after all, maybe the diary is a dead thing, is a death.

I left the doctor's office after that session to meet John, but all the way downtown on the train I was scribbling almost incoherently. As if I were in a sort of mystical state. I didn't want to find out that our intimacy was illusory, either had not happened at all or was gone. We had been together, united, one might say; I was not struggling against the immobility, the fear of him, the unrealness of him, him as a figure in a chair, a figure outside my world: more simply, I was suddenly not isolated from him, nor he from me.

Three days later, he began by asking if I still felt any excitement, if the intimacy of the days before had survived, and I had to say no, it had been lost in the intervening motions of life. I was excited at first, and disbelieving, and frightened too; the measure of my feeling was in the fact that I had to write it down immediately: nothing was real until it was recorded. In the three days he seemed to have become even more convinced of how important this might be, while I didn't dare to think about it. And then it came

back in a kind of rush: that what I had wanted all my life
was going to be realized. The literal sharing of myself, of
what I had always thought of as more myself than anything
else: more than any act or spoken words or relationship.
These things had all been carried on, carried out, in the
diary.

If he came to see, to read, my diaries, I thought, he
would become, even more vividly, intensely, one with me—
with my diaries, what I had always (though with periods
of doubt) considered to be my real self, a self that communicated better on paper than in talk, in real life. He had
denied that so central part of me; finally he was admitting
that there might be truth in what I was in front of the
typewriter. At the thought of his visit I felt both doubt and
anticipation.

> What will you see in it? Events and people I have
> never told you about. But what emotionally will you
> see, what in terms of what you see now, the child-
> woman who sits before you, on the edge of the chair
> or on the floor, hanging her head, fixing her eyes on
> the carpet or on some point of the wall or the win-
> dow and so rarely on you. Pacing, backed against the
> bookshelf, or wrapped in the curtains . . . cold . . .
> crying. Inside desperately reaching for you, while the
> arms, crossed, clutch her own body, containing: deny-
> ing you sitting back in your black chair with your
> legs crossed. And you lean forward, you come to her
> on the floor or behind the curtain, and for a moment
> she submits to her longing. And goes stonily from the
> room.

I thought obsessively about what was happening, had
happened between me and the doctor; about the meaning
of the diaries, and him and the diaries; and, concretely,

how it might be possible to read the huge mass of them. Sometimes eager for his visit, sometimes wishing it would never be, yet always conscious of him, writing now for him—or perhaps I had always been writing for him:

> You: I suppose there has always been a You in some embodiment or other, the person to whom the letter was addressed. It always surprises me, in the mornings particularly, to see you as a body, a real, live person, for the way I think of you is not in human terms. You are a kind of all-powerful spirit, haunting and possessing and obsessing me, present even when I am engaged in other things.
>
> At the end of tomorrow you wait for me, and with that light I live. But there is the accompanying fear that it/you is a myth, a dream: a fabrication to soothe my shattered self. The fear of having to sit in a stony silence and then leave with nothing: the tears, the anxieties remaining trapped inside. Please, I cry, take them from me. I sit on the edge of the chair tensely longing to throw myself at your feet, a suppliant crying out for mercy, for saving. I suppose in some way you know this, but are powerless to take from me what I do not know how to give. To tell me who I am when I give you no clue. The only constancy is the black words on the page, and in your recognition of that I am to find some hope, some consolation, if there is any.

I became very engrossed in my new apartment. I couldn't wait to move, but first I needed to clean, paint, sand the floors, make arrangements about the phone, the electricity, the gas. In the first apartment I had had after Susan and I split up, other people had taken care of everything, and I had made no attachment to it. Now I wanted to do everything myself: to be sure that it would be *my* house. Finally, at the end of March, I was there: it was white, airy, it had a view of streets and, where two of the streets divided, a triangular space with pieces of rusty sculpture in it. I did not think I was going to close the door and die, as I had feared the other time. Yet it also seemed to be taking me away from myself: there was always something to do, to put away or arrange or fix. My diary seemed to be a record of the apartment, of its taking shape. Settled, I thought: will I ever be settled? And then: If it can happen physically perhaps it can happen mentally.

I had always felt that writing was what made sense of the days and nights, the so-called experiences; their preservation in writing gave the illusion of their having actually happened, assured or reassured me that I was "living." Nothing was lived but the writing: nothing was quite real, or made sense, but this. But as I became involved in my apartment—in an external life, as it seemed to me—I became confused. I wished to be left alone, feeling that the old gap between outer and inner lives was more acute than ever. Was there really a gap, were there really two lives, two selves? That's what crazy people say: "It wasn't me who broke that bottle; it was someone else, some part of me that has no relation to the me of every day. I don't know who made the slice in that arm, etc." It was a temptation— more than temptation, a deep sensation, an instinct—to think of the person who slashed and smashed as someone distinct. The coming together of doctor and diaries would be the coming together of two selves; it ought to be accomplished symbolically, but in my world that was impossible: it had to happen concretely (like cutting). I was lucky in his understanding of that.

In my new apartment I was preparing, always, unconsciously, for the doctor's visit: I wanted him to come but I did not want it to be over. I unwrapped the broken-off base of a blue glass seltzer bottle; in it were more pieces of glass. I started to wrap it again, hide it, but stopped: I didn't want to be hidden. All my life I had pretended to hide but really I wanted to be known, discovered: that was another meaning of the doctor's coming to look at my diaries. But I was still anxious, afraid: "He takes me on, or in, but he also abandons me, every day. Every day I must go through being lost, and only sometimes found; and even when I am found it is only for what, in time, is the briefest moment, before I am sent out to the street again."

I felt paralyzed each time the thought broke in on me, in clear black and white, of his coming, seeing. For once, I thought, he will be the one to leave. But then I reminded myself that in the hospital it was like that: and it was terrible, his vanishing out the heavy door.

At last the doctor made his visit: we sat in my room with the bookshelves and he looked through my diaries, the ones from childhood where each page began "Dear Diary" and ended "love, Grace." So the idea of a diary's being a letter, and to someone, was already there. He brought a cake; we had tea. And when it was over I could hardly believe it had happened. What did he think? Was there someone here? Did he recognize her?

I had been left by him: abandoned. It was the way I had felt that summer when he came from his vacation to see me: the intensity was of abandonment, of being left or lost rather than of being found. The feeling of being in one world had existed—must have existed; but then it was destroyed by being cut off, and being cut off became the only experience. I did not regret his visit; only, I could not hold on to it.

Telephone calls were an attempt to mitigate the cutoff feeling. There were calls at certain times: Monday morning, for example, after the weekend; or at the end of the session on Friday he might say he would call Saturday, or Sunday, in the gap of the weekend. I dreaded these calls, and yet if they had not been made I would have felt abandoned; I hated them yet longed for them. I would say "I have nothing to say"; he would say, "Yes, this is what often happens." Or he might say "I said I would call." And then, enraged, I imagined him feeling that he was doing his duty, his job; fulfilling an obligation, without feeling. To him it's work, I thought; to me it's my entire life.

I always tried to picture him at the other end of the phone; and wished I could picture myself to him, but even if I had had the words they wouldn't have come out right. I gathered my bits of information but they seemed sparse, did not approach the picture of a complete life, complete self.

His self, being my self. If I had the details of him, did I then have the details of me? But the visit had had the opposite effect, of attaching me closer instead of separating me, and thus I seized on the details of his life, what time he gets up, what he has for breakfast, what he did last night . . . When I asked what he had seen when he came to visit, he said it was not a shadow but a whole living person, a house, rooms, in which he could later visualize me, which gave him a more complete picture, a more intimate sense of the person who comes four times a week to sit beside him. If he saw, that was supposed to help me see.

About a week after the doctor's visit, I dreamed about him and the subway: he was the driver, and I wanted to get on the train and go to the end of the line. The subway was my world, cut off from him, where he didn't exist and which he didn't know; but it was a container, holding, mother. Leaving his office in distress, if I could get myself to the train I would be all right; sometimes the two blocks to the station seemed impossible; sometimes he would drive me. I stood between cars and screamed into the tunnel until my voice was hoarse. I did ride trains to the end of the line; eventually I got to the end of every line. Still, what I mainly felt was loss: lost. Intimacy, unity were unrecapturable. I felt distant even from my apartment: despite its brightness, whiteness, spaciousness I did not know anymore that I was there: I seemed as isolated, as shut up as ever. I might have lived there all my life and did not live there at all.

Susan and I began, tentatively, to write letters: but what were letters after eight years of daily devotion? Now I was bound to the doctor in the same awful inextricable way; but it wasn't the same, he wasn't there, wasn't close enough. "You call me on the telephone and there is nothing to say. I say it and you say it. But then I am going to see you, the progression of suits and ties from day to day. Now it's dark and I am in a room of orange-lighted windowpanes: I could have told you that on the phone, in a voice fading into whispers because it could not form words for its detachment, its disembodiment. You are supposed to be its embodiment."

Again I tried by writing, by physically locating myself in both space and time, to make some agreement, some balance, some terms with myself. Let go the shell, find the core, some undisturbed place inside the body-covering. But I could dig and dig and in the end find nothing:

> I am not attached to anything, not complete myself, I
> am an unfinished product, a never-to-be-finished
> body of a woman: I am not always sure if there is a
> real feeling behind what I say or imagine, or if it is
> made up to satisfy an inner need for definition: for a
> story and a symbol. For a memory: it is memories that
> give one a sense of having lived, of having been;
> memories that can coalesce into what appears to be a
> person. The relics and signs of my grandparents
> around me force a sense of the past. Also the diaries

on the shelves, the papers lying on the tables.
Through pages and objects I search, but what I am
searching for is not to be found except in symbols
and signs and the images evoked by them; if I
could remain here endlessly, infinitely, I might find
or be found.

# Epilogue

(Dr. Nakhla)

Grace's psychotic core and her inner state of fragmentation broke through and lay there visibly and concretely between us when she smashed the pot holding the shredded newspaper. It was a hopeful moment for both of us: the sense of a starting place on the path of recovery. Grace wrote in her diary:

> I am holding on to him: What can you do with these shreds? . . . I look questioningly at him: Can I? He nods yes and I throw it. I never thought I could destroy anything I made; I could be careless but not deliberately, consciously destroy. It gives me a kind of hope that I can destroy the unliving, self-containing part of myself; but at the same time is the fear that

having once begun I will be unable to stop destroying.

In these words was her unconscious expression not only of
the fear of disintegration, or a breakdown that would never
end, but of hope that she might find in me what she needed
to make her feel whole. Her unconscious sense of hope was
also triggered by the feeling of aliveness kindled by her
violent and deliberate physical action. This "spontaneous
gesture," as Winnicott put it, was Grace's "True Self in
action." In the beginning, he says, the True Self "means
little more than the summation of sensorimotor aliveness."[1]

The therapeutic journey that evolved was a struggle
through primitive agonies of frightening force: disintegration, the sense of depersonalization, and Grace's feeling
that her center of gravity was located outside her, in the
holding care. It was a journey through a fear of madness
(Winnicott 1952). The clinical account tells how Grace and
I survived the severe regression, with its oscillations between states of oneness and of separateness; the uninte-
grated coexistence of intense feelings of love and hate; and
the dangers of suicide and murderousness, to reach the
beginning crystallization of her identity.

Some facets of my participation and the meaning of the
experience must be seen in terms of my own identity. This
treatment endeavor was certainly a unique and major departure from my usual style of clinical work, and I em-
barked on it in a very deliberate fashion. Knowing the
psychoanalytic literature, I was aware of the controversial
nature of my approach, forewarned but by no means pre-

1. For a discussion of Winnicott's concept of the True Self, an
idea that cannot be fully described, see "A Theory for the True Self"
(Bollas 1989b), "The Birth and Recognition of the 'Self'" (Pontalis
1981a), and "The Hopeful Return to the Past" (Lomas 1973b).

pared for the full impact of its complexity and dangerous-
ness.

As I have indicated, I brought to the decision to change
my treatment approach the sense of failure I had experienced in the outcome of one of my control cases during
analytic training. My conviction that I needed to attempt a
treatment along the principles described by Winnicott was
reinforced by his last significant paper (1969b), in which
he reiterated his warnings about the sense of futility re-
sulting from a therapy conducted in the false self or defensive organization. He emphasized the need to address a
patient's psychotic core, which disrupts his vital sense of
self. Winnicott was not referring here to the type of patient
with a frank psychosis in the clinical psychiatric sense. He
writes:

> In such cases the psychoanalyst may collude for
> years with the patient's need to be psychoneurotic (as
> opposed to mad) and to be treated as a psychoneu-
> rotic. The analysis goes well, and everyone is
> pleased. . . . But in fact the patient knows that there
> has been no change in the underlying (psychotic)
> state and that the analyst and the patient have suc-
> ceeded in colluding to bring about a failure. (1969b,
> p. 187)

My interest and motivation also derived from a more
personal source: this treatment relationship seemed to offer
an opportunity for experimenting with new techniques and
for expanding my knowledge and experience—for making
a journey of self-discovery. Winnicott, in a paper written
when he was engaged in research analyses of borderline
patients, wrote:

> Psychoanalytic research is perhaps always to
> some extent an attempt on the part of the analyst to

> carry the work of his own analysis farther than the
> point to which his own analyst could get him. (1947,
> p. 96)

Classically trained analysts are not known to be daring
or innovative in their analytic techniques. Analysts often
remark, however, that there is a discrepancy between what
is actually practiced and what is disclosed, because of their
reluctance to expose the true nature of their work to their
colleagues. During psychoanalytic training, candidates are
taught, through suitably selected control cases, to follow an
established analytic process and technique. In subsequent
years, as their clinical careers evolve, they may be reluctant to take even minor departures from such a scheme—
departures through which they may find the freedom
to learn from their patients and to develop their individ-
uality.

A year after qualifying as a psychoanalyst with the
British Psycho-Analytical Society, I moved to New York;
my treatment with Grace commenced a few years later. In
New York, distant and isolated from the society I belonged
to, I held on to my identity as an analyst from the British
school and compensated for the distance by studying the
work of British analysts (a number of whom had been my
teachers but whose work was not taught in my training
curriculum). My analytic identity was reinforced by my
teaching this work to psychiatric residents over a number
of years. At the same time, I was aware that the therapy I
was undertaking with Grace was not based on my established identity, and that not being in a position to be an
integral part of and a participant in the activities of a psychoanalytic society may have allowed me greater freedom
to pursue my own way.

Searles (1966–67) speaks of the individual identity that
evolves from the foundation of a symbiotically based iden-

tity—the world with which the self is at one. In his later writing (1979b) he expresses the conviction that in work with the borderline psychotic patient the analyst must far outgrow the traditional classical-analyst identity. The analyst, Searles believes, needs to utilize his sense of identity as a perceptual organ and to preserve his analyst-identity to face the extremely intense and perplexing feelings that will dominate his actual identity.

Little (1951), in the same vein, states that with psychotic patients the therapist's countertransference through an identification with the patient's id can do all the work in making contact with the patient. She emphasizes, however, that the analyst's paranoid and phobic attitude toward the inevitably intense feelings that will be aroused constitutes the greatest danger in the countertransference. She adds that the analyst's authenticity and his honest recognition of these intense feelings are essential to the analytic process.

Similarly, I was left to my intuition in trying to understand and find my responses to Grace's intense feelings and behavior, which often frightened and confused me. Her courage and perseverance, however, had a single-minded quality that fortified my commitment to our struggle and sustained my overall belief in the direction we were taking. Still, I never felt assured of a safe outcome. There was always an uneasiness, an anxiety and uncertainty about her recovery—and the very real danger that she might kill herself.

Grace and I both were struggling—each in a distinct way—with our identities. At risk for me was my personal identity as well as my identity as an analyst. The treatment setting—a shared office suite—imposed a strain on my work: there was the fear that my patient's behavior would disturb or intrude on my colleagues' work environment and that my unorthodox form of practice would be viewed dis-

approvingly. In spite of the complexities and fears I encountered, I was reluctant to consult colleagues, fearing
that they would not support the course I was taking. (In
fact, this was my experience when I did consult a senior
colleague a few years after Grace was out of danger and
her therapy was proceeding in a more settled and ordinary
fashion. He strongly disapproved, feeling that there was no
justification for the extreme parameters and dangers to
which I had subjected my patient. He was also disinclined
to explore any research value that could be derived from
this clinical work.) The threat of malpractice suits, which
has increasingly burdened and hampered clinical work, did
not seem to preoccupy me; it was not an issue with Grace
or her family.

I always felt that Grace and I were on the same side; I
also felt that we were joined by her family, who not only
invested in our struggle but also dealt courageously with
their own pain and fears. Because of their invaluable participation and most unusual devotion, Grace and I have
dedicated this book to them.

# Clinical Appendix

(Dr. Nakhla)

Over the first eighteen-month period of Grace's treatment, during which I saw her once a week, I was baffled and deeply frustrated by her total nonengagement in my analytically oriented approach.

Grace was representative of a large category of sicker patients who, although they turn in increasing numbers to psychoanalysis for help, are unable to use our ordinary techniques. All too often such patients are lost to the designation "unanalyzable" and relegated to a second-rate form of treatment. Winnicott, in his 1954 paper "Metapsychological and Clinical Aspects of Regression within the Psycho-Analytic Set-Up," warned that the era in which psychoanalysis could limit itself to the classical technique was steadily drawing to a close. He addressed this problem by grouping cases according to the technical equipment they would require from the analyst. Grace was one of those patients, as Winnicott put it,

> whose analyses must deal with the early stages of emotional development before and up to the establishment of the personality as an entity, before the achievement of space-time unit status. The personal structure is not yet securely founded. . . . The accent is more surely on management and sometimes over long periods with these patients ordinary analytic work has to be in abeyance, management being the whole thing. (p. 279)

A great deal has been said since then about the expanded scope of psychoanalytic treatment. Anna Freud (1969) was clearly opposed to and skeptical about such an expansion of psychoanalytic treatment:

> Any attempt to carry analysis from the verbal to the preverbal period of development brings with it practical and technical innovations as well as theoretical implications, many of which are controversial.
>
> What strikes the observer first is a change in the type of *psychic material* with which the analysis is dealing. Instead of exploring the disharmonies between the various agencies within a structured personality, the analyst is concerned with the events which lead from the chaotic, undifferentiated state toward the initial building up of a psychic structure. This means going beyond the area of intrapsychic conflict, which had always been the legitimate target for psychoanalysis and into the darker area of interaction between innate endowment and environmental influence. The implied aim is to undo or to counteract the impact of the very focus on which the rudiments of the personality development are based. . . .

There is, further, the question whether the transference really has the power to transport the patient
back as far as the beginning of life. Many are convinced that this is the case. Others, myself among
them, raise the point that it is one thing for pre-
formed, object-related fantasies to return from repres-
sion and be redirected from the inner to outer world
(i.e., to the person of the analyst); but that it is an
entirely different, almost magical expectation to have
the patient in analysis change back to a prepsycholog-
ical, undifferentiated, and unstructured state, in
which no divisions exist between body and mind or
self and object. (pp. 38–41)

It was precisely these earliest disturbances of psychic structure which interested Winnicott and were central to Grace's
disordered sense of self. Psychoanalysts in the mainstream
still view the development of severe regressive phenomena
during analytic treatment as undesirable and dangerous.
They caution that significant technical departures to pro-
mote or respond to such regression in an attempt to further
the treatment process are potentially harmful and can put
the analyst at risk of acting out in a way that is reminiscent
of Freud's "wild analysis" (1910).

Rather than pursue this important and controversial
issue of technical departures, I shall instead turn to Grace's
treatment as one contribution to the challenging problem
of such patients. It involved the management of a severe
regression, which was at times hazardous and difficult to
handle but eventually proved effective in bringing about
psychic change and emotional growth. The clinical and
technical aspects of this regressive analysis illustrate well
the principles set forth by Winnicott.[1] On the basis of the

1. Influenced by Winnicott's work, Little (1981), Khan (1974),
Milner (1969, 1987), Green (1975, 1986), Stewart (1989, 1992), Bollas

clinical data from his research analyses of schizoid and borderline patients, he reconstructed a model of the mother-infant relationship. (This work extended over a quarter of a century, from 1945 to 1971, and is contained in a number of publications.) He also developed the theoretical concept of a "false self," which results from premature reactions to early environmental failure. This false self is a defensive organization that copes with the external world, protecting and hiding the true self. Winnicott became convinced that a regression experienced in the analytic setting can re-create this failure and facilitate a re-emergence of the true self.

This therapeutic regression could be seen as being dependent on the patient's latent capacity for regression in the face of the threat of chaos. It is not a simple reversal of progress; rather, there is now hope for a reversal of the original failure through the analyst's active adaptation to the patient's needs in the analytic setting. The treatment, a "self-cure," then becomes a "healing process," which originates in the split-off true self and may allow the patient to see himself and the world in a new way. Winnicott (1958a) expresses this poignantly when he says that the patient reaches "a *place* from which to operate," a place where the patient gets in touch with the basic self, and "what happens from here is felt as real" (p. 290).

He also (1963d) emphasized that such a regressive treatment should not be equated with Alexander's (1948) idea of the "corrective emotional experience," in which the an-

(1987, 1989a), and Ogden (1986, 1989) have extended our technical and theoretical understanding of therapeutic regression. R. Gaddini (1990) discusses Winnicott's ideas of therapeutic regression and gathers some of the opinions about it expressed in Winnicott's letters (Rodman 1987).

alyst assumes a specific role to differentiate himself from the patient's parents.[2] In fact:

> The operative factor is that the patient now hates the analyst for the failure that originally came as an environmental factor, outside the infant's area of omnipotent control, but that is *now* staged in the transference.
>
> So in the end we succeed by failing—failing the patient's way. This is a long distance from the simple theory of cure by corrective experience. In this way, regression can be in the service of the ego if it is met by the analyst, and turned into a new dependence in which the patient brings the bad external factor into the area of his or her omnipotent control. (p. 258)

As Grace let go of her defenses, she collapsed into a breakdown, and we both struggled to endure and to find our way through endless experiences of intense anxiety, rage, destructiveness, and confusion. Constant thoughts of the hardships that Winnicott (1954b) described in the analysis of a severely regressed patient fortified my courage and resolution. His statements, however, were put in general terms:

> The treatment and management of this case has called on everything that I possess as a human being, as a psychoanalyst, and as a paediatrician. I have had

2. This treatment is, of course, a "corrective emotional experience" but not in accordance with Alexander's concept, which has been justly criticized or dismissed by many analytic writers. For a cogent presentation of the nature of the curative experiences that can be found in the context of the treatment relationship, see Casement, "The Meeting of Needs in Psychoanalysis" (1991a), and Lomas, "A Second Attempt at Parenting" (1990a).

to make personal growth in the course of this treatment which was painful and which I would gladly
have avoided. (p. 280)

Thus, although his ideas were of great value to my clinical
work with Grace, his writings, lacking specific accounts of
his behavior in managing his patients' vulnerabilities and
needs, provided me with little help in keeping my bearings
during the many difficult and bewildering times we went
through.

Misgivings about whether the whole treatment was ill
considered and doubts about my technical skills were
heightened by my awareness of Balint's work on therapeutic regression and his cautions against the hazards of what
he called a malignant regression syndrome. In fact, the
clinical picture of Grace's treatment rapidly developed all
the characteristics of Balint's concept (1968, p. 146).

Balint, a pioneer in the treatment of severely regressed
patients, believed, like Winnicott, that a patient can use the
analytic setting to find new solutions for the effects of an
early environmental failure.[3] The aim in the regression is a
*recognition*, and the patient attempts to "reach and find
himself" in what Balint called a new beginning. He contrasted this benign type of regression with the malignant
type, where the patient aims at *gratification* of instinctual
cravings by an external action. He warned that in these
circumstances the analytic atmosphere becomes charged
with intense wishes and destructive despair and usually

---

3. Balint and Winnicott have been viewed as continuing in the
path first set by Ferenczi, with his active technique and therapeutic
optimism and his departure from contemporary classical technique,
which was a source of tragic disagreement with Freud, in the early
1930s. (See Stanton 1991, Dupont 1932, Hoffer 1991; see also Balint
1968, for his views of the traumatic effect and repercussions of this
disagreement on the psychoanalytic community.)

escalates to an unmanageable and disappointing termination.[4]

Winnicott's thinking on the nature of the therapeutic regression is best reflected in his distinction between regression to primitive instinctual wishes and fantasies and his idea of needs. He put it succinctly:

> It is proper to speak of the patient's *wishes*, the wish (for instance) to be quiet. With the regressed patient the word wish is incorrect; instead we use the word *need*. If a regressed patient *needs* quiet, then without it nothing can be done at all. If the need is not met the result is not anger, only a reproduction of the environmental failure situation which stopped the processes of self growth. The individual's capacity to "wish" has become interfered with, and we witness the reappearance of the original cause of a sense of futility. (1954b, p. 288)

Winnicott (1963a, 1963b) similarly differentiated the "object-mother" of instinctual aim and fantasy from the "environmental mother," who holds and handles the baby and adapts to its needs.

Grace's breakdown during her treatment occurred when she abandoned her "false caretaker self" in the hope that I would contain her and meet her needs so that she might emerge alive and real. Her regression took her back not only to infancy but to the earliest environmental failure, where there had been a break in her "continuity of being." In her earliest memories, annihilation had occurred, and her psychotic anxieties concerned her sense of existence and identity. Little (1966) states that to analyze these areas

4. For a further discussion of the technical problems of malignant regression as conceptualized by Balint, see Stewart (1989) and Bacal (1981), who present divergent views.

of psychotic anxieties means going back to a not yet per-
sonalized state, and that means experientially going
through annihilation and death, and coming forward again,
but differently (p. 484).

Little's ideas, as outlined in her papers "On Delusional
Transference" (1958) and "On Basic Unity" (1960), proved
of immense value in helping me to understand and manage
Grace's psychotic states and transference manifestations.
(Little has also written an account of her own analysis with
Winnicott, including the way her psychotic anxieties were
managed during a regression [1985, 1990].) Little says that
patients like Grace need to regress to a state of one-hundred-
percent dependence. The transference has a delusional nature; the patient, assuming the analyst to be magical, both
deifies and diabolizes the analyst. The patient unconsciously is in a state that Little terms basic unity: one of
undifferentiatedness and absolute identity with the analyst.
Little points out that this psychotic transference and unconscious delusion is, of course, in only part of the patient's
psyche; otherwise the patient would be totally insane. In
other areas the patient is aware of the separateness and
reality of the analyst.

Little emphasized the importance of body happenings
in those areas where the delusion of basic unity is operative
because

> the patient is to all intents and purposes literally an
> infant, his ego a body ego. For him, in these areas,
> only concrete, actual, and bodily things have meaning
> and can carry conviction.
>
> Discharge, and consequent differentiation, comes
> through some body event—a movement, a scream, sal-
> ivation, etc.—by means of which some kind of bodily
> contact with the analyst occurs. Through the repeti-
> tions of such events the patient comes gradually to

recognize the difference between his body, his sensations, and his emotions, while those of the analyst are discovered as separate from his. The event has concerned two people, and the patient discovers himself as a person who has moved, screamed, etc., in relation to another person, whose separate existence, experience, movements and responses can also be recognized. The delusion breaks up, recovery begins, and relationship becomes a possibility.

The body events may become the interpretations. Verbalization then becomes the second stage in a two-stage process, both stages being necessary for real insight to be attained, but the second being only effective as a result of the first, i.e., of the bodily happening. (1960, p. 378)

Weinshel's and Searles's views of Little's work are helpful in arriving at a critical judgment of her complex clinical and technical concepts. Weinshel (1985), in his review of Little's book *Transference Neurosis and Transference Psychosis* (1981), says that although the chapters "On Basic Unity" and "On Delusional Transference" are considered to be among her chief contributions, they were problematic for him:

I believe that my relative dissatisfaction stems from the essentially inevitable distance between the *observable* clinical data and the proposed formulations to explain those data. I say "essentially inevitable" inasmuch as Dr. Little is dealing with extremely archaic material, pathology, and "structure" (really lack of structure). She describes patients who want to establish not just a symbiotic relationship with the analyst, "but rather one of total identity with the analyst and of undifferentiatedness with him.". . . I confess that I

did not achieve a comfortable understanding of the
concepts advanced by the author. (pp. 148–49)

Elaborating on his difficulties with these theoretical intricacies, he says:

These issues and dilemmas are not, of course, limited
to the work of Margaret Little. They arise almost inevitably when psychoanalysts write or talk about very
disturbed patients and archaic psychological structure
and organization. At times it appears that every colleague who describes his work with such individuals
has his own vocabulary, his own conceptualization of
psychopathology and his own "map" of the primitive
psyche.

Little and Searles (1963), however, are two analysts
who have described similar ideas in the concepts of "delusional transference" and "transference psychosis," and
each has acknowledged the value of the other's ideas in the
development of his own work with psychotic patients.

Searles (1973, pp. 335–37), in his response to Little's
discussion of his paper "Violence in Schizophrenia,"
writes:

I know of no other writer besides Little who ac-
cepts as fully as I do that what I term a phase of therapeutic symbiosis (or, in Little's phrase, of undifferentiatedness) is essential in successful therapy [with the
psychotic patient]. It is powerfully strengthening to
me to read her statements. . . ."I agree entirely with
Searles that the reactions brought about in the therapist are of prime importance. The ability to allow his
ego boundaries to dissolve temporarily—to let himself
become merged with the patient, and to permit reality
and delusional or hallucinatory experience to become

indistinguishable—is the only route by which real
contact, understanding, and ability to share in an experience can develop." (pp. 361–62)

Searles goes on to say that he also fully agrees with her
next comment: "But equally important are the ways in
which boundaries can be re-established, and the speed and
progression of the resynthesis when it is appropriate."
Searles acknowledges that Little's writings have been most
helpful to him in this latter connection.

Little (1967), in her review of Searles's *Collected Papers on Schizophrenia and Related Subjects* (1965), states
that she has been a longtime admirer of his work and that
nothing he describes is completely outside her own experience. She emphasizes, however, that a main point of difference lies in his use of "symbiosis" and "the undifferentiated state" as synonymous terms. She writes:

> To me they imply different things, "symbiosis"
> implying that at least one stage of division or differ-
> entiation has occurred, whereas "the undifferentiated
> state" (which I have elsewhere called "Basic Unity")
> implies *homogeneity*; and a radical change occurs
> when the *factual*, objective *unreality* of homogeneity
> and the objective *reality* of paradox have to be recog-
> nized. It is this change and disillusionment—the
> "moment of truth" that is feared by both patient and
> therapist, as equated with death or annihilation—
> "non-being"—and it is both towards, and away from
> this change that every schizophrenic and borderline
> patient is striving ambivalently, in life and death
> struggles, now with and now against his therapist.
> (p. 117)

One of the critical issues in terms of departures from
the usual analytic method is the complex question of phys-

ical contact with a patient during periods of deep regression. Weinshel's (1985) comments in his review of Little's work are pertinent. He does not so much present us with his skepticism or concerns about the dangers of such interventions as set before us the important challenge of the evaluation and closer study of the effectiveness of such interventions. He writes:

> I have avoided taking any explicit position on whether and where Dr. Little has been doing psychoanalysis or psychotherapy. In part these distinctions do not appear to bother Dr. Little; she is more concerned with helping the patient as best she can without regard for what others may feel about "what" it is she may be doing. I find it difficult to fault her on that score. In part, my reluctance reflects a hesitation in asserting that *another* analyst is or is not doing psychoanalysis, especially when that statement is based on very limited data, especially from a longitudinal point of view.
>
> I am cognizant that such a stand smacks of a kind of timidity if not cowardice; and this is especially pertinent in regard to both trying to teach and trying to understand what "we" mean by psychoanalysis. While it may be impossible to come up with foolproof and absolutely convincing criteria for what I or what "we" decide falls within psychoanalysis, it is nevertheless more than just an abstract academic issue to insist that as a profession we do devote ourselves to the not always congenial task of establishing, testing, and clarifying these criteria. For me, at least, it is most difficult to accept that physical contact with a patient—except under the most unusual circumstances—can be seen as part of the psychoana-

lytic process. Yet I do not believe that it is appropriate to dismiss cavalierly as unanalytic those instances of physical contact that come up in Little's work until we understand much more fully than we do currently the psychoanalytic significance and impact of such interventions. (p. 150)

Rosenfeld (1969), in his paper "On the Treatment of Psychotic States: An Historical Approach," points to a dichotomy in the theoretical and technical approaches to psychotic patients. One trend, exemplified by the work of Klein and her followers, particularly Rosenfeld, Segal, and Bion, relies exclusively on verbal transference interpretations without any change in the analyst's attitude or the introduction of technical parameters. A second group of analysts considers that transference interpretations are ineffective and believes that a change in the usual analytic attitude is necessary to connect with the patient so as to cure the effects of an environmental failure and bring about a resumption of psychic growth. In Winnicott's words, "Psychosis is an environmental deficiency disease" (1965, pp. 135–36, 256).

Benedetti (1975), in his paper "The Experience of the Body in Schizophrenia and Borderline Patients," reminds us of the centrality of the early body ego in the evolution of the sense of self and of how the relation of the psychotic patient and his body is disrupted. He describes a patient who wanted to be, and believed she was, a pure spirit, without a body; as she became connected to her therapist, she started to fear (but unconsciously to hope) that her relation to her therapist would become more and more "bodily." Benedetti illustrates how the patient used the relationship with the therapist as a substitute for the relationship to her own body.

Sechehaye (1956) is explicit in describing the importance of the procedures of "contact and physical care" that are directed at the body ego of the very regressed schizophrenic and through which contact can be established. She describes a "pre-transference" phase with such patients (comparable to Searles's "out-of-contact" phase), in which, she believes, the analyst needs to take all the initiative to establish a relationship. She views the "schizophrenic transference" that evolves not as a real transference but as a "graft-transference" (an "emotional graft"): the patient transfers onto the analyst his desires, his deep needs, and his hope of finding an ideal mother. She draws a similarity between the emerging struggle of the real person hidden behind the psychosis and Winnicott's idea of the true self and the false self.

Searles (1963) believes that physical contact can be helpful in the therapy of the schizophrenic patient but also emphasizes that to help the patient become subjectively alive "one must be unafraid of functioning as the transference representation of the subjectively unalive parts of the patient's self, or as the very early perceived attributes of the mother, before she had emerged as a whole and alive human being in the perception of the infant." He also cautions against the anxieties that compel the therapist "to reassure himself of his own living humanness, his own capacity for feeling, by a dramatically 'curative' employment of physical contact with the patient. . . . It is ostensibly the trembling and frightened patient who is being helped by the therapist's reassuring touch; covertly the patient is thereby reassuring the therapist of the latter's own capacity for life and lovingness" (pp. 700–01). Casement's (1982) paper "Some Pressures on the Analyst for Physical Contact During the Re-Living of an Early Trauma" presents a detailed clinical account and discussion of how the analyst's refusal to hold the patient's hand in dealing with an intolerable anxiety helped in the resolution of a brief near-psychotic transference episode.

Fox (1984) discusses Casement's clinical material at some length in his paper "The Principle of Abstinence Reconsidered." He advocates applying the technical concept of abstinence not as a "rule" but, rather, as a "principle," using the discriminating guideline of what the analyst must provide, as well as withhold, in order to further the development of an analyzable transference.

In my therapeutic approach with Grace, I felt that my function was to provide a caring and protective setting and to sustain a deep connection with her that would enable her to formulate her needs in her struggles to feel real and alive and to move toward differentiation and becoming a whole and separate person. In responding to her bodily and emotional needs, the holding environment I provided was active and real rather than what Modell has described as "symbolic actualization" (1984d; 1990, pp. 38–43). My responses involved physical contact and care, relating through movement and action in and out of the office, and tolerating life-threatening behavior even though it put Grace through much agony and danger. As I have said, to help in managing this perilous course I prescribed medication—an anti-anxiety drug (Librium) and a low-dose neuroleptic (Navane)—and I found a continuous source of support in a hospital staff that was prepared to accept my treatment endeavor and to back me at any time by taking over and providing a holding situation.

During a later phase, Grace's family (her parents and two sisters) played a significant part in our struggle. They shared in the responsibility of providing a loving and caring environment. Federn (1952, pp. 120–21) emphasized not only the importance of establishing and sustaining a positive transference in the analytic treatment of the psychotic patient but the fact that no psychoanalysis of a psychotic can be carried through without the loving care and assistance of a family member or friend. In fact, the deep regressive relationship that Grace formed with her mother in turn contributed to the work of re-creating and helping her tolerate the original failure and a new dependency. This brings to mind an interesting parallel with Mahler's model of the treatment of the psychotic child, which attempts to involve the mother in the provision of a "corrective symbiotic experience" (1968, pp. 184–95). The family's participation in Grace's care and in family-therapy sessions also brought about changes in family interactions and relationships, particularly in the areas of poor "levels of differentiation" and defensive "emotional cut-offs" (Bowen 1978).

There is an extensive literature on the interactional nature of the analytic relationship as a "two-person psychology" in which analyst and patient influence each other. Searles more than anyone else has written about the therapeutic effects on the analyst and, going further, hypothesizes that the patient's "therapeutic strivings" toward the analyst are an important element in the treatment situation. In his lengthy and rich paper "The Patient as Therapist to His Analyst" (1975) he places special emphasis upon "the psychotic patient's therapeutic effort to enable the mother (and analogously, in the analytic context, the analyst) to become a whole and effective mother (= analyst) to him" (p. 459).

At the height of her destructive behavior and delusional transference, I remarked to Grace: "I don't know why I go on seeing you. The experience must mean something to me, though I couldn't say what. We're in it together." I can now understand these remarks not only as an expression of my "*objective* countertransference hate" (Winnicott 1947) but also as a recognition of the therapeutic strivings in the experience for *both* of us. I can now also gratefully acknowledge Grace's help in enabling me to become more whole and enriched by being more in touch with my primitive self. As Winnicott (1945, p. 150n) put it: "We are poor indeed if we are only sane."

# References

Abelin, E. (1971). The role of the father in the separation-individuation process. In J. B. McDevitt and C. F. Settlage, eds., *Separation-Individuation: Essays in honor of Margaret Mahler*. New York: International Universities Press.

Adler, G. (1985). *Borderline psychopathology and its treatment*. Northvale, N.J.: Aronson.

Alexander, F. (1948). *Fundamentals of psychoanalysis*. New York: Norton.

Anthony, E., and Benedek, T., eds. (1969). *Parenthood: Its psychology and psychopathology*. Boston: Little, Brown.

Arvanitakis, K. (1987). The analytic frame in the treatment of schizophrenia and its relation to depression. *Int. J. Psa.* 68: 525–33.

Bacal, H. (1981). Notes on some therapeutic challenges in the analysis of severely regressed patients. *Psa. Inq.* 1: 29–56.

Balint, M. (1968). *The basic fault.* London: Tavistock.

Barnes, M., and Berke, J. (1971). *Mary Barnes: Two accounts of a journey through madness.* New York: Harcourt, Brace, Jovanovich.

Benedetti, G. (1975). The experience of the body in schizophrenia and borderline patients. In 1987.

———(1987). *The psychotherapy of schizophrenia.* New York: NYU Press.

Bergmann, M. (1988). On the fate of the intrapsychic image of the psychoanalyst after termination of the analysis. In *Psychoanalytic Study of the Child.* Vol. 43. New Haven: Yale University Press.

Bollas, C. (1987). *The shadow of the object.* New York: Columbia University Press.

———(1989a). *Forces of destiny: Psychoanalysis and the human idiom.* London: Free Association.

———(1989b). A theory for the true self. In 1989a.

Bowen, M. (1978). *Family therapy in clinical practice.* New York: Aronson.

Boyer, L. B., and Giovacchini, P., eds. (1990). *Master clinicians.* Northvale, N.J.: Aronson.

Braudy, S. (1977). A day in the life of Joan Didion. *Ms.*: February.

Casement, P. J. (1982). Some pressures on the analyst for physical contact during the re-living of an early trauma. *Int. Rev. Psa.* 9: 279–86.

———(1991a). *Learning from the patient.* New York: Guilford.

———(1991b). The meeting of needs in psychoanalysis. In 1991a.

Chasseguet-Smirgel, J. (1986). *Sexuality and mind.* New York: NYU Press.

———(1992). Some thoughts on the psychoanalytic situation. *J. Amer. Psa. Assoc.* 40: 3–25.

Deutsch, H. (1942). Some forms of emotional disturbance and their relationship to schizophrenia. In 1965.

——(1965). *Neurosis and character types*. New York: International Universities Press.

Didion, J. (1969). *Slouching towards Bethlehem*. New York: Dell.

Dupont, J., ed. (1932). *The clinical diary of Sandor Ferenczi*. Cambridge: Harvard University Press.

Eigen, M. (1983). Dual union or undifferentiation? A critique of Marion Milner's sense of psychic creativeness. *Int. Rev. Psa.* 10: 415–28.

Federn, P. (1952). *Ego psychology and the psychoses*. New York: Basic.

Fox, R. (1984). The principle of abstinence reconsidered. *Int. Rev. Psa.* 11: 227–36.

Freud, A. (1969). *Difficulties in the path of psychoanalysis*. New York: International Universities Press.

Freud, S. (1910). "Wild" psychoanalysis. In *Standard edition* 12: 1–82. London: Hogarth.

Gaddini, E. (1982). Early defensive fantasies and the psychoanalytic process. *Int. J. Psa.* 63: 379–88.

——(1987). Notes on the mind-body question. *Int. J. Psa.* 68: 315–29.

Gaddini, R. (1978). Transitional object origin and the psychosomatic symptom. In S. Grolnick, L. Barkin, and W. Muensterberger, eds., *Between reality and fantasy*. Northvale, N.J.: Aronson.

——(1986). I precursori dell'oggetto e dei fenomeni transizionali. *Rivista di Psicoanalisi* 32: 281–95.

——(1987). Early care and the roots of internalization. *Int. J. Psa.* 14: 321–32.

——(1990). Regression and its uses in treatment. In L. B. Boyer and P. Giovacchini, eds., *Master clinicians*. Northvale, N.J.: Aronson.

Giovacchini, P., ed. (1972). *Tactics and techniques of psychoanalytic therapy*. Northvale, N.J.: Aronson.

Green, A. (1975). The analyst, symbolization, and absence in the psycho-analytic setting. *Int. J. Psa.* 56: 1–22.

———(1986). *On private madness.* New York: International Universities Press.

Greenacre, P. (1958a). Early psychical determinants in the development of the sense of identity. *J. Amer. Psa. Assoc.* 6: 612–27.

———(1958b). Toward an understanding of the physical nucleus of some defense reactions. *Int. J. Psa.* 39: 69–76.

Grolnick, S., Barkin, L., and Muensterberger, W., eds. (1978). *Between reality and fantasy.* Northvale, N.J.: Aronson.

Guntrip, H. (1968). *Schizoid phenomena, object relations, and the self.* New York: International Universities Press.

Hoffer, A. (1991). The Freud-Ferenczi controversy—a living legacy. *Int. Rev. Psa.* 18: 465–72.

Kafka, J. S. (1969). The body as a transitional object: A psychoanalytic study of a self-mutilating patient. *Brit. J. Med. Psych.* 42: 207–12.

Khan, M. (1974). *The privacy of the self.* New York: International Universities Press.

Klauber, J., and others (1987). *Illusion and spontaneity in psychoanalysis.* London: Free Association.

Laing, R. D. (1960). *The divided self.* London: Tavistock.

LeBoit, J., and Capponi, A., eds. (1979). *Advances in the psychotherapy of the borderline patient.* Northvale, N.J.: Aronson.

Little, M. (1951). Countertransference and the patient's response to it. *Int. J. Psa.* 32: 32–40.

———(1957). "R"—The analyst's total response to the patient's needs. *Int. J. Psa.* 38: 240–54.

———(1958). On delusional transference (transference psychosis). *Int. J. Psa.* 39: 1–5.

———(1960). On basic unity. *Int. J. Psa.* 41: 377–84.

————(1966). Transference in borderline states. *Int. J. Psa.* 47: 476–85.

————(1967). Review of Harold Searles, *Collected papers on schizophrenia and related subjects* (1965). *Int. J. Psa.* 48: 112–17.

————(1981). *Transference neurosis and transference psychosis: Toward basic unity.* Northvale, N.J.: Aronson.

————(1985). Winnicott working in areas where psychotic anxieties predominate: A personal record. *Free Associations* 1: 9–42.

————(1987). On the value of regression to dependence. *Free Associations* 10: 7–22.

————(1990). *Psychotic anxieties and their containment.* Northvale, N.J.: Aronson.

Little, M., and Flarsheim, A. (1972). Early mothering care and borderline psychotic states. In P. Giovacchini, ed., *Tactics and techniques of psychoanalytic therapy.* Northvale, N.J.: Aronson.

Lomas, P. (1973a). *True and false experience.* New York: Taplinger.

————(1973b). The hopeful return to the past. In 1973a.

————(1990a). *The limits of interpretation.* Northvale, N.J.: Aronson.

————(1990b). A second attempt at parenting. In 1990a.

McDougall, J. (1989). *Theaters of the body.* New York: Norton.

Mahler, M. S. (1963). Thoughts about development and individuation. In *Psychoanalytic Study of the Child.* Vol. 18. New York: International Universities Press.

————(1968). *On human symbiosis and the vicissitudes of individuation.* Vol. I: *Infantile psychosis.* New York: International Universities Press.

————(1971). A study of the separation-individuation process. In *Psychoanalytic Study of the Child.* Vol. 26. New York: Quadrangle.

Mahler, M. S., and McDevitt, J. B. (1982). Thoughts on the emergence of the sense of self with particular emphasis on the body self. *J. Amer. Psa. Assoc.* 30, 4: 827–48.

Mahler, M. S., Pine, F., and Bergman, A. (1975). *The psychological birth of the human infant: Symbiosis and individuation.* New York: Basic.

Milner, M. (1969). *The hands of the living God.* London: Hogarth.

———(1987). *The suppressed madness of sane men.* London: Tavistock.

Modell, A. (1968). *Object love and reality.* New York: International Universities Press.

———(1976). The "holding environment" and the therapeutic action of psychoanalysis. *J. Amer. Psa. Assoc.* 24: 285–307.

———(1984a). *Psychoanalysis in a new context.* New York: International Universities Press.

———(1984b). On having the right to a life. In 1984a.

———(1984c). Self-psychology as a psychology of conflict. In 1984a.

———(1984d). Interpretation and symbolic actualizations of developmental arrests. In 1984a.

———(1990). *Other times, other realities.* Cambridge: Harvard University Press.

Ogden, T. (1986). *The matrix of the mind.* Northvale, N.J.: Aronson.

———(1989). *The primitive edge of experience.* Northvale, N.J.: Aronson.

Pontalis, J.-B. (1981). *Frontiers in psychoanalysis: Between the dream and psychic pain.* New York: International Universities Press.

———(1981a). The birth and recognition of the "self." In 1981.

Reich, A. (1958). A special variation on technique. *Int. J. Psa.* 39: 230–34.

Rey, J. H. (1979). Schizoid phenomena in the borderline. In J. LeBoit and A. Capponi, eds., *Advances in the psychotherapy of the borderline patient*. Northvale, N.J.: Aronson.

Rodman, F. R. (1987). *The spontaneous gesture: Selected letters of D. W. Winnicott*. Cambridge: Harvard University Press.

Rosenfeld, H. (1969). On the treatment of psychotic states: An historical approach. *Int. J. Psa.* 50: 615–31.

Searles, H. F. (1961). Phases of a patient-therapist interaction in the psychotherapy of chronic schizophrenia. In 1965.

———(1963). Transference psychosis in the psychotherapy of schizophrenia. In 1965.

———(1965). *Collected papers on schizophrenia and related subjects*. New York: International Universities Press.

———(1966–67). Concerning the development of an identity. In 1979a.

———(1975). The patient as therapist to his analyst. In 1979a.

———(1979a). *Countertransference and related subjects*. New York: International Universities Press.

———(1979b). Countertransference as a path to understanding and helping the patient. In 1986.

———(1986). *My work with borderline patients*. Northvale, N.J.: Aronson.

Searles, H. F., Bisco, J. M., Coutur, G., and Scibetta, R. C. (1973). Violence in schizophrenia. In H. F. Searles, *Countertransference and related subjects*. New York: International Universities Press.

Sechehaye, M. A. (1947). *Symbolic realization*. New York: International Universities Press.

———(1956). The transference in symbolic realization. *Int. J. Psa.* 37: 270–77.

Stanton, M. (1991). *Sandor Ferenczi: Reconsidering active intervention*. Northvale, N.J.: Aronson.

Stern, D. (1985). *The interpersonal world of the infant*. New York: Basic.

Stewart, H. (1989). Technique at the basic fault regression. *Int. J. Psa.* 70: 221–30.

————(1992). *Psychic experience and problems of technique.* London: Routledge.

Tolpin, M. (1971). On the beginnings of a cohesive self. In *Psychoanalytic Study of the Child.* Vol. 26. New York: Quadrangle.

Weinshel, E. (1985). Review of Margaret Little, *Transference neurosis and transference psychosis* (1981). In *J. Amer. Psa. Assoc.* 33 suppl.: 146–51.

Winnicott, D. W. (1945). Primitive emotional development. In 1958a.

————(1947). Hate in the countertransference. In 1958a.

————(1949a). Mind and its relation to the psyche-soma. In 1958a.

————(1949b). Birth memories, birth trauma, and anxiety. In 1958a.

————(1950). Aggression in relation to emotional development. In 1958a.

————(1951). Transitional objects and transitional phenomena. In 1958a.

————(1952). Anxiety associated with insecurity. In 1958a.

————(1954a). Withdrawal and regression. In 1958a.

————(1954b). Metapsychological and clinical aspects of regression within the psycho-analytic set-up. In 1958a.

————(1955). Clinical varieties of transference. In 1958a.

————(1956). Primary maternal preoccupation. In 1958a.

————(1958a). *Collected papers: Through paediatrics to psychoanalysis.* New York: Basic.

————(1958b). The capacity to be alone. In 1965.

————(1960a). The theory of the parent-infant relationship. In 1965.

————(1960b). Counter-transference. In 1965.

————(1960c). Ego distortion in terms of true and false self. In 1965.

——(1962). Ego integration in child development. In 1965.

——(1963a). The development of the capacity for concern. In 1965.

——(1963b). Communicating and not communicating leading to a study of certain opposites. In 1965.

——(1963c). From dependence toward independence in the development of the individual. In 1965.

——(1963d). Dependence in infant-care, in child-care, and in the psycho-analytic setting. In 1965.

——(1965). *The maturational processes and the facilitating environment.* New York: International Universities Press.

——(1969a). The mother-infant experience of mutuality. In E. Anthony and T. Benedek, eds. *Parenthood: Its psychology and psychopathology.* Boston: Little, Brown.

——(1969b). The use of an object and relating through identifications. In 1971a.

——(1971a). *Playing and reality.* New York: Basic.

——(1971b). Playing: Creative activity and the search for the self. In 1971a.

——(1971c). Creativity and its origins. In 1971a.

——(1971d). Mirror-role of mother and family in child development. In 1971a.

——(1971e). Interrelating apart from instinctual drive and in terms of cross-identifications. In 1971a.

——(1971f). Letter to Mme. Jeannine Kalmanovitch. *Nouvelle Revue de Psychoanal.* 3: 47–48.

——(1972). Basis for self in the body. *Int. J. Child Psychother.* 1 (1): 7–16.

——(1974). Fear of breakdown. *Int. Rev. Psa.* 1: 103–107.

——(1988). *Human nature.* New York: Schocken.

Wright, K. (1991). *Vision and separation.* Northvale, N.J.: Aronson.

# Author
# Index